Praise for Kenny W
Effortless Mastery

Kenny Werner has written the definitive book on how musicians can attain freedom and be an inspiration to their audiences.

There is a Master Musician inside every one of us, however we understand that concept, and when musicians release their fears, they can tap into that wellspring and become a powerful force.

In the same way the musician can adopt a practice regimen aimed squarely at virtuosity without apology.

These duel concepts of focus and inspiration, preparation and performance, are so well documented in Kenny's book, *Effortless Mastery*.

Many years ago I heard him playing with Toots Thielemans and observed that Kenny embodied many of the qualities he wrote about. There are many musicians that manifest that level of virtuosity and inspiration, but Kenny has the rare ability to explain it so clearly, as he does in his book. Step by step, he describes ways of walking out of the shadows of self-limitation and into the possibilities of joy and self-expression in music.

There's a reason this book is so popular from generation to generation. The concepts are universal and timeless.

I myself am a fan of Kenny's music and ideas.

—QUINCY JONES, foreword from *Effortless Mastery*

I was going through a terrible time with the horn.

A separation and divorce has me stuttering through the instrument and aside from not having any fun playing I lost all confidence on the trumpet that I started playing when I was eight years old. I had prior commitments to perform with my group in Europe and I struggled and faked it as best I could. Then I became aware of the great trumpet teacher, Carmine Caruso, who never played trumpet but understood the art of teaching and treating all students as individuals. I first met him at a hotel in New York City and I liked him immediately. After a while, I asked what he thought I was doing wrong on the trumpet. He was not willing to tell me, saying that I wouldn't be able to change my problem that quickly. So I ordered a few drinks from room service and got him to confess. He said that I was trying to play the trumpet with my mouth open. His method was likening the musician to an athlete. He taught the physics of playing the instrument, and that the musician is the instrument, and the trumpet is just "a piece of plumbing." Carmine likened musicians to athletes and the need to synchronize the muscles to timing, similar to the rhythm of a boxer hitting a punching bag. Little by little things started to open up for me on the horn, but my confidence was still down. I always felt that I had my own sound but I wanted to stretch out and play more improvisational music.

Then I read Kenny Werner's amazing book *Effortless Mastery*. I reached out to find his number to see if I could take a few lessons from him. At first he didn't believe that I was calling him. I guess he was relating to my past history and that I also produced one of his favorite albums by my dear friend and genius composer, Michel

Colombier, called, Wings. We made an appointment and I met him at his home and spent the most interesting time as he demonstrated to me how you can express yourself musically, from a spiritual point of view. To demonstrate he sat at the piano and before he played a note he closed his eyes and in a very quiet way it seemed like he was channeling or meditating. He then started playing the piano with notes that seemed to be coming from a very deep and honest place. Then we did some of his exercises and we played music together. His method helps to free the fear and the critical inner demons that block our ability to find our own unique feel, instead of analyzing what we do in relation to our favorite musicians. I wanted to find my own personal voice as a jazz artist. Kenny and *Effortless Mastery* were the keys for me. His book is tremendous. I love the feeling of inventing music as I go along and Kenny's method helped me to break the BS barrier. The music I was looking for is all about freedom, the freedom to express myself and my deepest feelings. Improvisational music needs preparation, accepting and trusting your instincts, and you are only as good as all the negative energy you can eliminate from your performance. Kenny Werner's book, *Effortless Mastery,* can open that door and get you in touch with your own uniqueness. The book's approach helped me find my own personal expression. *Effortless Mastery* is simple, direct, perfect . . . and profound.

—HERB ALPERT, foreword from *Effortless Mastery*

Becoming *the* Instrument

Also by Kenny Werner

Effortless Mastery

Becoming *the* Instrument

Lessons on Self-Mastery from Music to Life

KENNY WERNER

SWEET LO PRESS

New York

Copyright © 2021 by Kenny Werner
All rights reserved.

No portion of this book may be reproduced in any way without the
express written permission from the publisher. For information,
including permission to reproduce this book or any portions contained
therein, please contact the author by visiting www.kennywerner.com.

Published by Sweet Lo Press. First edition January 2022.

Library of Congress cataloguing-in-publication data is on file with the
U.S. Copyright Office.

PAPERBACK: ISBN 979-8-9850750-0-7
EBOOK: ISBN 979-8-9850750-1-4

Co-edited by Kenny Werner and Reggie Marshall
Book and cover designed by John Lotte
Cover and title page photographs by Jacky Lepage

Manufactured in the United States of America

KATHERYN   *In love and gratitude for what she taught me in too short a time period. I'm still working on it, my sweet darling.*

LORRAINE   *Standing by me for all time. The biggest heart I've ever known. Supreme caretaker to animals, plants and artists.*

BONNIE   *My best friend. Hopefully this book will do so well I can bring that cardboard box into her office!*

GURUMAYI CHIDVILASANANDA   *My teacher, a fully realized master who loves me. She patiently guides me towards self-love or love of the "Self," and she welcomes me with all her heart.*

Contents

Preface

When I wrote my first book, *Effortless Mastery,* it was an acknowledgment of a kind of special knowledge I seemed to possess since early childhood. You could even call it a kind of wisdom, an understanding of something so clear, that I thought everyone understood the same thing. It's very much like perfect pitch. It was my second teacher who noticed that I wasn't practicing the pieces he assigned, but just "remembering them" after he left. One day he asked me to turn my back and name the notes he was playing. This I did with great ease. He turned me around again, looked me in the eye and said, "Do you realize that you have perfect pitch?"

I said, "Perfect pitch, what's that?"

He said, "The ability to recognize the note or notes being played without seeing what they are."

I replied, "You mean you can't do that?" It was incredulous to me that everyone couldn't simply tell what notes were being played. For me it was as obvious as colors. The knowledge I had was so simple and clear, I didn't realize it was something not commonly known.

I was a precocious child who had no patience to learn anything. However, I still had a tendency to pontificate about things I knew nothing about. I would sense ideas that were untested. This was a failing of mine but also a strong point. Many of those ideas turned out to be right.

The "knowledge" I was streaming usually had to do with creativity, or how to be creative. I knew how to do this easily.

Being creative and, in fact, entertaining was in my genes. When I was only three years old, I went to dance school. At my parent's parties I would get up on a chair and sing. I would also do impressions of the television personalities of the day. I remember getting really high from being in the spotlight, a fact that I was ashamed of later in life when I was supposed to be an "artist." I don't think I really comprehended what an artist was, I liked to entertain. I still do. Whether it was singing, dancing or telling jokes, I really enjoyed the delight on people's faces when I performed. I got off on having an effect on people.

Like having perfect pitch, I didn't know where these creative instincts came from, they were just there, allowing myself to be free, to be silly, and not to be burdened by self-analysis, at least where music was concerned. But later on in life I realized that others did not always know these things. For instance, I never thought music was that important. People still gasp when I say that out loud. But when I compared it to food, water, shelter, breathing, etc. it was obviously a secondary consideration. This information turned out to be very useful in avoiding much of the drama associated with performing. I have my own dramas, to be sure, but they have rarely involved going on stage to do what I just "do." I have felt similarly unfazed whether playing at Carnegie Hall or Carnegie Deli across the street. I was always kind of detached. This offhand attitude seemed like a negative early on, but much later it became a positive. After having a couple of very influential teachers in and after college I began to see this attitude in another context. More and more I could step out of my own way and watch myself play. I hope the gift of this knowledge will help the reader ascend in any endeavor of choice.

When performing with others I sometimes noticed their eyes were closed. At first, I assumed it was because they were deeply into the music and sometimes, they were. But sometimes they were enveloped in simply trying to play well. I would observe this from a rather detached place and began to notice that this great caring about one's performance did not help, but rather inhibited the flow of creativity. Of course, we all care, but it was not helpful to care as one was about to play. I used to like to think, "No one has ever played piano before me." It certainly wasn't helpful if, as I was about to play, the words "Keith Jarrett" popped into my head. That usually caused me to overplay and run out of gas.

All this made more sense to me later in life when I began to study Eastern thought, yoga, Zen, Kashmir Shaivism, the wisdom of the Upanishads and Sufi philosophy. For example, in the Bhagavad Gita (which by the way, is 18 chapters and 700 verses that resides in the middle of an even larger work, the Mahabharata), the whole text is devoted to a point in the story where Arjuna, the hero, is compelled to go to war with competing factions in his royal family. He is about to enter into battle beset by doubts and sorrow and doesn't want to go through with it; he knows he will have to kill uncles and cousins. Suddenly, his chariot driver reveals himself to be Lord Krishna. What follows is 700 verses on detachment. I found this reference many years after experiencing it. I then understood that wisdom didn't always come from books. Sometimes comes it from within, like a great lake where anyone may refresh themselves.

I continued to have profound experiences and people started to ask me to explain what I was doing. That led to teaching, lecturing and eventually writing my first book, Effortless Mastery. I also seemed to have a natural ability for verbalizing what was going on in my head. I was more of a sportscaster, being able to call the plays in my brain. Three different therapists have told me as much.

When I started to teach, I noticed that I could tell what was going on in other people's heads too. In Effortless Mastery, I detailed the kind of rationalizations, deceptions, negative messages, procrastinations and other ploys the mind goes through that stand in the way of great practicing and playing. Many people told me when they read the first part of the book that it was as if I was a fly on the wall in their apartment. "How does he know that's exactly the way my head works?" Again, it seemed to be a gift that I didn't have much to do with. But it was immensely helpful to people who felt that I understood their frailties. I did, but not from music. I had compassion for young and old musicians who, ironically, were blocked by their hearts desires because I had the same atrophy in other areas of life. Knowing how the mind's attachments can limit dreams and possibilities is as important as anything else in the equation. There is much information about that in this book. To master oneself, usually involves principles that are physical, mental, and spiritual. The metaphysical is hiding in the physical world. We must find it! Therein lies our greatness. Transformation doesn't come without homework.

Since 2014, I've been Artistic Director of the Effortless Mastery Institute at the Berklee College of Music. Teaching what I always knew innately and turning that knowledge into courses has given me a lot more ways to express freedom. I was surprised to find that so many people in other walks of life were getting lessons from my first book. People in business and even in the military were emailing fantastic letters of gratitude. Becoming The Instrument widens the scope intentionally. I hope the ideas herein will be easily transferrable to all walks of life and any passion one has for accomplishment and mastery. The success may depend on being able to master one's self. In that we all find common ground.

It's important to note that this book will be reckoning with, commenting on, doubting, supporting, mocking, and rapturously drenched in spirituality. It could not be otherwise. How can one begin to write about the state of Becoming The Instrument and avoid the subject of "Who is playing?" Being an instrument is like being a piece of furniture. As attractive as that sounds to some of us who think too much, there really would be no point in discussing the virtue of such a state if there wasn't a belief that some power would play the instrument. That belief alone locks us into the reality of "a greater power." It could be God, Jesus, Buddha or Charlie Parker. Or it could be the 11th percent of our brain. Who knows? Who cares? (I know that many do!) What "It" is or if It even exists is irrelevant, for in the end it is the power of our faith that drives humans to superhuman accomplishments. Once we accept that premise, then we realize there could be an untapped and never-ending reservoir of creativity, power, courage, and good, old-fashioned smarts available if we are willing to surrender our own sense of self and become a channel for The Source. Then, all the other implications come into play. Every time there is a synonym for what one might call God, I'll capitalize the word, as in "Jesus" or "Thelonious Monk," or even "I." (For after all, who is "I?")

If you're expecting reverent language, I'm just a Jew from Long Island, New Yawk. (Intentionally misspelled.) I was raised on and schooled by television. My lifelong journey has been to replace "numbness" with True Connection. My learning of deeper concepts comes more from movies and television than anything scholarly. You'll see that throughout the book. I've finally accepted that about myself. It's important for me to reveal that because I would like you to understand; this connection is available to anyone.

The kingdom of heaven lies within YOU!

I will be funny at times, or at least I will think so. Some of it will be my own personal journey. I find it a fascinating journey of accepting and appreciating more and more of who I truly am, the good and bad. If I speak in my authentic voice, I can speak about anything and it still sounds like me.

You might wonder what I'm doing writing a book like this. I wondered the same thing this morning. I don't have the knowledge. I didn't study the crossover elements of neurology, quantum physics, not much theology, psychology, and the like. This is certainly not a scholarly work. I have had one thing that many of the scholars have not—the experience. I do one thing that puts all those things into motion—play the piano. This is my validation. I do it . . . almost every time I play. Many artists do, but I've always had the weird ability to express it in words, define it, even invent exercises for others to practice it. Whatever "it" is. I'm writing this book in the hopes that you can have this experience dependably when you perform, no matter what the nature of that performance is, no matter what instrument you use.

There will be some phrases that will piss some people off. *It's only music, or, something as insignificant as playing a musical instrument.* I'm hoping they will be seen in the context of the possibility of even greater liberation. But in the spirit of that liberation I'll say, whatever.

As in my first book, *Effortless Mastery,* there are meditations. There is also a recording reciting the meditations because how can you read a meditation that starts with "Close your eyes." They are there to read as a means of reinforcement or before listening. One thing I've learned in my own life, we need as much help as we can get. The meditations, and this book in fact, aim at giving you moments when you recognize that your own Higher Self, your own Great Being—You, lies within. Then if you can let that being play, write, create, program, swing a golf club, whatever—you can surrender to your own *greatness!*

So, I apologize and I don't apologize for the blatant spirituality in this book. I assure you it is coming from a healthy distrust of, if not resentment towards organized religion and at least a firm agnostic view in defining The Source. To me, just being able to describe it using one's art is part of the essential importance of art itself. It's an irreverent look at reverence. After all, you don't want to just worship God, you want to keep him entertained as well!

Be forewarned:

I love italics.

––––––

Becoming *the* Instrument

Prologue ■ A Story

Once there was a musician who studied a great Yogic path under a great spiritual master. For years he was following the path and in his mind he was sure that he was mostly fumbling, not moving forward towards the goal. Every year his teacher would give a message for the year to work on, and every year the message would vaporize by March.

In 2016, he received a message about *Supreme Joy*.[1] One thing he was grateful for was the infinite compassion of his teacher to include the words "move towards becoming." She recognized that even after all the exposure her devotees had to limitless knowledge and wisdom, the struggle would continue.

Certainly, this "Teflon" musician felt resistant to any amount of wisdom. The effect of it would always be fleeting and the delusion would reappear. But he kept practicing, kept it alive in his psyche and in his heart. It seemed that

1   Move with Steadfastness Towards Becoming Anchored in Supreme Joy,
     New Year's Message 2016, Gurumayi Chidvilasananda

finally, some of the obstacles to his joy were beginning to fray. Although going through much turmoil in his life, the last part of the message, *Supreme Joy,* he knew well. Since he was a boy, if he put one finger on a piano, he commonly experienced *Supreme Joy.* He had a neural pathway that equated the touch of the instrument to joy and self-love; he was loving mistakes, not very attached to how he played; nor even the importance of music. He knew that the whole purpose of music was to please himself and allow it to pour through.

He had even authored a book that liberated many of its readers, but it didn't necessarily mean that he could apply its wisdom to the rest of his own life. The light seemed to shine only when he was making music. In his book, he had identified a place beyond the conscious mind simply as *The Space.* There was a process that involved four steps to be practiced at one's instrument.

The first step was for the musician to empty him—or herself of thoughts and *go into The Space.* There was nothing new about the idea of going into *The Space,* other than the simplicity of the term itself. In fact, the idea was as old as humankind. The innovative element for a musician is that he or she would enter *The Space* while *touching their instrument.* In this space, one is drained of all desires and relinquishes control of their playing. One of the profound benefits of that awareness can be freedom from inhibitions.

But in his life, he was the opposite, dark, attached, self-hating, and unforgiving when making mistakes—all the things he easily avoided when playing music. This was the great quandary of his life; how to imbibe the joy he experienced automatically on the piano bench when he was off it.

Then one day, while chanting an extremely long chant of 182 verses, he began to feel integration. It wasn't a new idea to him but it suddenly connected. Although he had practiced meditation for twenty-six years, he didn't practice too regularly. So that tool, that new neural pathway, had never been forged. But he had a well-worn path to this space through the touch of his instrument.

Normally, while chanting this very long chant, he would do what he did with the rest of his life—become anxious for it to be over in order to get to the next activity. He didn't have to know what that next activity was; all he knew was that he was always in the wrong place, had to finish that activity and get to the next place. It was the fabric of his life-long discontent. This time however, while chanting he thought about going into *The Space* and then something happened. Instead of counting the verses and watching the time, he connected with every verse, every word. There was no time. He was just in the moment. Instead of feeling low energy from the onslaught of thoughts, he felt great energy and alertness from being connected to only one moment, *the* moment.

After he finished the chant, he continued to think of the first step, continued to put himself in front of the instrument, hands down, in *The Space*. Suddenly the integration between life and music was happening. If he extended his hands into the air as if playing the piano, the balance to his mind was immediate. His life started to feel easier, more joyful, less dramatic, and as focused and self-generous as he was with his playing. It seems the musician had finally found what he always had in music: joy, love, laughter, ease, detachment, loving one's own mistakes, and allowing a higher force to speak through his actions like it did through his music. It seemed a very fortuitous time to finally start his second book, the first one in twenty years, an activity that he suddenly had infinite energy for. He also started writing music again for the first time in a few years.

Now he just hoped the world would continue to exist so he could live to enjoy it.[2]

2   This book was started October-November of 2016

1 ■ *The Space*

**You must be nothing but an ear that hears what
the universe of the world is constantly saying
within you.**

/ Rabbi Dov Baer of Mezritch /

I want to talk about *"The Space."* For that I will quote myself.

**There is a place inside each of us where perfection
exists. The genius, God, lives there.
All the creative possibilities of the universe are
to be found there.**[1]

Some call it the Super Conscious Mind, some call it Universal Mind, every culture and religion have a name for this part of our awareness. Neuroscientists are discovering more and more how it actually works. It is how many feel in communion with God. I use a nondenominational term; *The Space.*

---

1 *Effortless Mastery,* P. 177

Popular terminology for *The Space*

Synonyms: *Universal Consciousness, Universal Mind, Holy Spirit, Holy Ghost, Oneness, Luminosity* (Not the website!), *Go with the Flow, Sweet Spot, Hashem* (Jewish sweet spot, Danish anybody?), *Locked In, In the Groove, Swinging, Follow the Inner Voice, Mindfulness, Possession* (can be wonderful if possessed by the right energy, scary if not!).

> "From this space, there is great compassion and great love, as well as great detachment. A person becomes the supreme enjoyer, observer and doer. His involvement in life is total. He fully participates in the world, yet is not ensnared by it. There is no fear, because he is not attached to the results of his actions. Practice takes no patience, since there is no burning need to reach the goal. There is simply the celebration of the doing, the learning, the achieving and the enjoying. To be sure, he experiences the entire range of emotions, but is not attached. Therefore, he can live his life and make his moves in harmony with his inner self and the outer universe. He frequently receives intuition about what to do next and he follows it fearlessly. Paradoxically, detachment causes his actions to have great purpose and result in great success. The abundance of the universe tends to rain on such a person; however, if it does not, that too is all right."[2]

Here I will quote another great philosopher:

Doing nothing often leads to the very best something.
/ Winnie the Pooh[3] /

---

2   *Effortless Mastery,* P. 50
3   Well, you know who that is!

The whole concept of *Effortless Mastery* rests in this one simple and universally agreed upon idea: **trying gets in the way of doing**. I have often started my master classes for musicians with this question, "Think about a time when you really needed to sound good, how did you sound?" I might paint the picture for them. "You had an important recital, or "jury" (I'm on a one-man crusade to get rid of that word!). Someone you were playing with or who came into the room you really wanted to like your playing. How did you play?" Most of the students *and teachers* look at each other nervously with a little smile, and then look back at me and say "bad" or "terrible" or simply give me a thumbs down. Then I ask, "Now think about a time when you really didn't care. Perhaps you had a couple of beers or you were playing with friends who loved and accepted you. For some reason you were duped into not caring—how did you play then?" Addressing the older players in the audience I might say, "Or you were playing a bar mitzvah and no one was listening."

Almost all of their faces would brighten as they said, "Better!" Then I would make a joke. "OK then, the master class could be over right now. You just learned the most important lesson in your life. All this time you thought that if you just tried harder, cared more or beat yourself up a bit more you would respond by playing better. Now you know, by your own experience, to play better you need to care *less!* Now that you know that, you're never going to care again, right?" This statement always produces laughter. Why? Because even when you realize that an action or old habit does nothing for you and you should release it, you can't. Ah, *there's the rub!*

Many who are well versed in neuroscience, psychology, neuropsychology, psychopharmacology, religion, and New

Age-ism may have more knowledge, but *all of us* can relate to this. Our mind forms habits, usually from very early in childhood, which leads to patterns of thought, which leads to habits later in life that we would not choose if we were *free to choose.*

A musician may be well versed in New Age vocabulary, meditate regularly, practice Tai Chi, Qigong, yoga, even music therapy, and say, *"I now surrender to the Grand Poo-Bah of the Aqua Gel of Consciousness and release all negative beliefs as I welcome my abundance* . . . or some such verbiage. But in parenthesis, they're saying: *(and then I'm really gonna play my ass off!)* and that attachment undermines the whole thing!

You see, once one decides to be a musician, the inevitable question begins to dog them, *Am I a good musician?* As they attempt to answer that question more and more, their practicing becomes more rushed, more fear-based, and their playing, more inhibited. The truth is once one is hung up on being a musician, they'd rather surrender a body part then surrender the need to *sound good!*

Why? Because if they play bad, they're going to *feel bad about themselves.* It's one thing to say, "I love myself, I am worthy", rather than "I just played badly." The hole most of us fall into is that if we play badly, *we feel less valuable as a person* and that is a *spiritual issue.* I don't subscribe to the notion of sin very much, but to devalue one's life for something as *insignificant* as how one plays an instrument, *that's a sin!* (This idea pisses off people!)

Music therapy is an interesting topic. So many musicians who have gone into it originally wanted to be performers. Very often, they could never get over performance anxiety, and then they found music therapy. Those people often tell me they were in bondage until they did music therapy and now, they've become free. I'd respond, "Well, you didn't have to give up performing to do this. When you're playing in Carnegie Hall, *just do music therapy!*" (Boy, that gets some quizzical looks!) You see, it's the *mindset* that frees us. When they do music therapy it's about *helping someone else,* not, *"How good do I sound?"* Many music teachers report they play much better when demonstrating to a student than when they're performing. There's an ancient Sanskrit saying, *"In the mind, bondage, in the mind, liberation."* It all depends on your mindset.

Take the indigenous peoples of the earth. (In the United States we call them Native Americans. Of course, that is not what they call themselves.) They were aware of the conscious mind and used it only as needed. They knew what it took to plant, to hunt, to build a teepee, to negotiate with other societies and clans. But they were most attentive to *The Space,* the Great Spirit, what nature was saying to them, who was speaking to them from the sky, or communication with ancestors. Most so-called "civilized" societies have completely lost that awareness through the presumptions of religion and, yes, even science. It causes us to miss what a butterfly is trying to tell us when it flies around our head or lands on a flower. We don't know the answer to these questions, perhaps we can't find the answers, but we can *listen for the answers. That's The Space.* Being willing to *listen to the silence.* If praying is talking to God, then meditation is surely *listening* to God, who may be expressing Himself/Herself/Themself in *silence.* (Will someone please give us language for multi-gender possibilities and put me out of my misery?)

More to the point, though American Indians may have used their intellect to figure out the process of building a home or creating a weapon, the actual work would then be done *from The Space*. That is to say, with *one-pointed focus* on the task, with patience, and without thought. This is my image of *The Space*:

> I'm sitting on the floor of the ocean. It is colorful, quiet, and for purposes of this image—clean. I feel my body connected to the water and therefore, to all animate and inanimate objects. Now I look up and see the water's surface. I see driftwood, beer cans, underwear, etc. floating by on the surface. I see it but I'm not touched by it. I am down here at the bottom, safe, still, connected.

As for the garbage floating on the surface, that's the conscious mind.

Properties of the conscious mind and *The Space*

From the Conscious Mind // **FROM *THE SPACE***

Expectations // **ACCEPTANCE**

Fear // **FAITH**

Bemoans what one doesn't have // **GRATITUDE FOR WHAT HAS BEEN GIVEN**

Attachments, needs, desires // **LUMINOUS FROM WITHIN, FREE FROM SUPPORT**

Jealousy // **GENEROSITY**

Doubts // **FAITH**

Self-Judgment // **SELF LOVE**

Separate from self and others // **CONNECTED TO ALL**

Competition with others // **COLLABORATION WITH OTHERS**

Afraid to take actions or make decisions. // **BLESSES BOTH AND MOVES ON**

Need to succeed // **ATTRACTS SUCCESS**

Worried about appearances // **SEES THE HIGHEST IN OTHERS**

Stress and strain // **SWEET REFRAIN**

Loses the groove // **IS THE GROOVE!**

That last one I tossed in for the musicians. The one before it I used because it rhymes!

As I said above, for musicians to enter this space they have to sacrifice their dearest possession, *the need to sound good.* When practicing *The Space,* the performance is of only peripheral concern. Since it's not always practical to sacrifice quality, the exercise is best done when one is not in performance, or "under the gun," so to speak. But the effects of such practice can *liberate* a performance. **Carelessness needs to be practiced!** It opens channels that "carefulness" could never attract. *(Fools rush in, where wise men never go . . .)*

One who performs his actions with detachment performs on the highest level. Watch YouTube videos of John Coltrane playing. (We can do that now!) Sometimes his eyes are closed or up in the back of his head while his chops are thrashing the tenor sax. He is not managing the gig, that's for sure, he is *receiving.* In fact, when he performed at the Newport Jazz Festival, which resulted in one of the most important jazz recordings in history, a little-known fact is that a lot of the audience did not like the music. His quartet with

McCoy Tyner, Jimmy Garrison, and Elvin Jones was at the height of its popularity. It was as if Coltrane was throwing it away and sticking it to his fans. But Trane heard something. So, did he obey his conscious mind? Did he *manage* his career? No! He followed The Voice and let the chips fall where they may. *That's The Space.* In doing so, he ushered in the next wave of jazz music! He went from one of the greats to immortality!

It's not just acting from *The Space* that will make one succeed. It is backed up with assiduous study. Practicing or studying from this space allows for focus and patience. Those qualities tend to bring one much closer to "mastery" of the language. John Coltrane is said to have practiced incessantly, all the time. One might say he was "lost in practice." (Or should we say, *Lost in Space?)* Practicing from the conscious mind tends to bring discontent, fear, and lack of concentration, uses up energy and makes one tired. Musicians often practice something for a while and then their ego-voice says, "I should know this by now." They play a gig or session and the thing they studied doesn't come out. The ego says, "I must be studying the wrong stuff. I need something else." Or it may even subliminally chant, *"I guess I'm not very talented."* But the problem is that our expectations (ego) make us think we had studied it enough. From *The Space* we would have simply observed that we hadn't studied it enough because *when we play it doesn't come out!*

And so it is with the acquisition of any knowledge. The ego-self says you've studied enough and then expects it to surface in your performance. You then berate yourself for not knowing it. (*Attention all golfers!)* On the other hand, you inhibit your performance by *expecting it to be there.* When we observe from *The Space* we observe with patience, not agitation, as from the mind. This is the truth, no matter what field you're in, no matter how much study is required.

The Space is that part of the mind where we may meet our own Higher Power, whatever we call it. Personally, I am becoming more and more persuaded that humans externalized our Ultimate Authority because we couldn't handle the amount of potential that lies within us. It may be that we create God in our own image. We know that we exist in a force larger than ourselves. That force can be seen all around us, in trees, in the sky, in babies, everywhere. But when we surrender our thoughts and focus on the "silence" we find that we join "The Force" that some call God. It's the way we access our own higher power within. We have *faith* that it is there, and we listen.

When I was in recovery I would go to different "A's" such as AA, NA, CA. They gave me my first rudimentary relationship to a "power greater than myself." Once at an NA (Narcotics Anonymous) meeting a guy came in and identified himself as a hitman. (CA, Cocaine Anonymous was mostly white-collar addicts. NA was a good deal rougher crowd!) Every time this guy came to the meeting he cursed, flipped everybody off and said F.U. to the idea of a higher power, or God. One day, a guy who was tougher than him looked him in the eye and said, "OK, buddy. You don't believe in a higher power? See this chair? Make this chair your higher power. Every day you come into this room, ask this chair to keep you sober." The guy took the suggestion. Each day he came in and asked the chair to keep him sober. But you could see that as the days passed, he seemed to have more and more respect, even *reverence* for the chair. Not only did he stay sober, but *he began to worship the chair!* In other words, he found God in that chair.

Now, did God enter the chair to connect with him? Was God always in the chair because He is everywhere? Or did the man contact the *spiritual* part of his brain because he imagined a God? *It doesn't bloody matter! (Pardon my English!)* He pretended there was a God in that chair and he began to find Him. I heard another guy in AA on tape say, "I looked for God everywhere. When I stopped looking, I found Him."

I reiterate, human beings might be absolutely awestruck at how much power lies within their own selves. It's an *inside job,* as they say in recovery programs. The light is always available, we just have to turn our face towards it, relax and bathe in its warmth and glow. That's *The Space!* "A true master is not just a master of technique or language, but of himself. He can sit serenely in the center of that space while performing his actions to perfection. This state of selflessness and absolute concentration is called *Samadhi* by Hindus and Buddhists. Meditation is the tool most often used to achieve this state."[4] Spirituality aside, there is a place for technique and a place to trust your technique and "go with the flow." Technique could be intellectual technique, such as a master of facts, systems or language. The argument for practice and technique is that when the body and mind are well trained, one can receive ideas from *The Space.*

In the coming chapters we will look at this relationship through several lenses. This space—or blessed state—is much easier to connect with than is generally thought. Let's take the quickest, easiest way to go into *The Space.* Try this now:

4   p. 79, *Effortless Mastery*

You're breathing. I'm sure of it. If you weren't, you wouldn't
be reading this book. You are breathing whether asleep or
awake, in joy or sadness, calm and meditative, or riddled with
thoughts. Through all conditions of life one thing is constant,
you are breathing. Now, just *notice* that you *are* breathing. Don't
exaggerate your breathing, don't deepen it or "tune in." Simply
notice *that you are breathing.* Don't think to yourself, "Wow,
something special is about to happen!" Don't think, "OK, we're
about to meditate," or that it could be profound in any way.
(The word "meditation" might be as prohibitive as the word
"bebop." Too well defined.) If you were sitting by the window
of a busy street there would be traffic outside, whether you
noticed it or not. How profound would it be if I told you to look
out the window and notice the traffic? Not very. Now regard this
suggestion with the same lack of importance.

   You were breathing already, simply notice that you are
breathing. Keep noticing that you're breathing. What happens?
You're not thinking. That's the trick. Somewhere in my lazy
man's guide to enlightenment I realized that I couldn't notice
my breathing and think at the same time. If I had thoughts, I no
longer noticed my breathing. If I continued to pay attention to
the breathing, there were no thoughts. I suddenly came into the
room—into the moment. Even if I had the thought, *"Wow! I'm no
longer thinking!"* I was no longer noticing my breathing.

When I do this with a room full of people, the atmo-
sphere in the room changes dramatically. Suddenly, there is
quietude, actually more than that, there is *awareness.* Often
there is more of a sparkle in people's eyes. It is amazing how
most people get it. That moment *is The Space.*

Once I was conducting a retreat on beautiful Cortes Island, off
the coast of Vancouver, one of the most beautiful places one

could ever see. As the participants pursued different workshops and retreats, the beauty of the island itself was one
of the great features. Some of them actually lived on Cortes
Island so, of course, they were well aware of its beauty.

Part of the program was watching ourselves breathe.
Before one of the breaks, I suggested they walk around outside and look at the beautiful surroundings, but instead
of focusing on nature, I asked them to watch themselves
breathe for the entire ten minutes. In other words, see what
they were seeing, but don't look. Look inside instead, and
watch the breath go in and out, like it always does when they
are not watching. Every one of them, including the natives
of the island, and said when they came in that although they
"saw" the ocean, the flowers, etc., that by focusing inside on
their breath they had never experienced the beauty as completely as they did on that break. They saw things they never
saw before. Isn't that stupendous? *Who woulda thunk it?*
Who would have thought that by focusing on the inside, the
breath, they would experience the outside as never before?
Imagine, while tuning inside, one merges with their environment outside *deeper than by trying to merge!*

It takes no effort whatsoever to slip into *The Space*,
the *God* part of your brain. There is no trick to entering
The Space. The problem is *staying in The Space.* Ah! Here is
the point of all somatic disciplines, such as holistic remedies, homeopathy, Bach Flowers, clinics, workshops, master
classes, retreats, The Mozart Effect, team-building, meditation, guru-disciple relationships, monastic living, runner's
high or just sitting in a chair—*they're all about staying in
The Space!* Its where the rubber meets the road! Of course,
the more one makes an effort to reach this region of the

brain, the more familiar he or she becomes with the terrain. Once a place is visited, one is more familiar with how to get there, and the more one revisits it, the more familiar it becomes.

It takes practice to move without thinking. It's scary, risky, but inspiration blossoms there. It might be more reasonable to practice it for short bits of time. It's better to be completely in *The Space* for two minutes than a compromised version for forty-five. Pretend, "I don't exist, I am sitting here but something else is using my eyes, ears, arms, hands, legs, feet, brain. Imagine if another, perhaps a Supreme Being or inspired force, was *thinking through you*. What thoughts you'd be filled with!

Ceasing to be a drop of water on the kitchen counter with an expiration date of 20 seconds, one lives forever as *a drop in the ocean*—an ocean of consciousness that retains the full power and flow of the ocean, but unlike the metaphor, retains all the qualities of its individuality. The individual is supported by its connection to the whole. It can succeed but it cannot fail! I tell musicians, *"If you play from The Space you might make a mistake but you could never go wrong."* The Space is something I've practiced or taught for more than thirty years. Anything practiced with that much repetition becomes an accessible tool of transformation. While the flow in my music or teaching is well established, as stated before, I've often had trouble integrating that wisdom into my life. I am remembering more and more to access the fruits of years of practice by telling myself to focus on my breath and go into *The Space*. It is a trigger to allow myself to revel in the moment. Fear of the future or regret of the past is so debilitating. In the process of *Effortless Mastery* one learns to enter *The Space*, move, and make choices from that space. I am now realizing that before I get sucked in by things I can't control, to stop fighting and go into *The Space*. Become empty and let action be done through me.

———————

Here's a story of dubious relevance to this chapter. *But The Space compels me! (The Exorcist?)*

> One of my favorite shows of all time was *Twilight Zone*. And one of my favorite episodes is "A Stop at Willoughby." If you get nothing else from this book, take my recommendation to watch that episode! An advertising executive is playing the game of business and ambition but is really not cut out for that life. The pressure of performance has given him a severe ulcer and depression. He gets on the train each evening to travel home to Connecticut where his wife has enough ambition for the both of them. The first night we travel with him he falls asleep on the train and has a dream. It's winter 1959 but when he enters his dream it's 1888 on a hot summer's day and he's on an old-fashioned train arriving at a town called Willoughby. It's a laid-back town with a town square, gazebo, an old buggy, and a couple of Huck Finn kids going fishing.
>
> It's not the relentless pace of New York City in the 1950s, but the gentle sway of life in the 1880s.
>
> The conductor comes through and announces, "Willoughby, next stop, Willoughby." Obviously disoriented, he asks the conductor where Willoughby is. The conductor says "Willoughby, sir? That's Willoughby right outside. Willoughby, July. It's 1888. Really a lovely little village. You ought to try it sometime. Peaceful, restful, where a man can slow down to a walk and live his life full measure."
>
> He gets up to walk out and there is a jarring motion on

the real train and he wakes up. At this point he thinks this was just the strangest dream. Upon arriving home, he explains the dream to his wife, who has no sympathy for him whatsoever. She thought she had married an upwardly mobile executive, not Huckleberry Finn. But as he tells her about his dream his mind clears and he marvels at the serenity he saw there.

The next day, we see him again buckling under the pressure and anxiety of his job. On the train to Connecticut again he falls asleep and has the same dream. He looks out the window of the old train and sees the town square. This time, a band is playing on the gazebo and people are gently walking through the park, the picture of tranquility. He gets up to go out and forgets his briefcase, *his one attachment*. He tries to get off the train and in the time it takes to make up his mind, the train starts up again. He's yelling to the conductor because he wants to get off at Willoughby. It turns out that he's yelling in his sleep on the real train to Connecticut. He pledges to himself that the next time he has that dream he's going to get off.

Then we see yet another day of disastrous dealings as everything goes wrong at work and his boss berates him mercilessly. In the quiet of his office, he calls his wife and tells her he's had enough. He can't take it anymore. As he's asking for her help, she hangs up on him. There he is, abandoned, condemned, and utterly without comfort.

He boards the train back to Connecticut, closes the blinds and prepares to have the dream. Sure enough, he falls asleep and again wakes up on the train just pulling into Willoughby. This time he looks happy, and he gets up and heads off the train. Seeing that he has his briefcase in hand, he lays it down on a seat. He's ready to leave the life he had and enter *The Space* and time of Willoughby. As he gets off, the kids who are going fishing greet him with a nice hello and he says he'll go fishing with them tomorrow.

Now he gently and happily walks into the town square. He's left the tyranny of his life and has been given the privilege of joining a gentler, kinder time and place where he belongs. He's ready.

Now, this story isn't the greatest parable because when he gets off the train in Willoughby, he's actually walked off a moving train in 1959 and committed suicide in his sleep, so . . . bad example? (lol) But there is a lesson here; living with the pressure of our own thoughts or dwelling in *The Space*: *"A place where a man can slow down and live his life full measure."* (The mindblower in the *Twilight Zone* is when the funeral home picks him up, the name on the rear door of the hearse says "Willoughby Funeral Home!")

Anyway, back to real life . . . or not?

It's time for us to get off.

Final thoughts

From this space one can imagine perfect lines, rhythms, harmonies effortlessly streaming out of the instrument, bypassing every obstacle.

Bring the practice of this perfect space to the forefront of your mind. Make the performances a peripheral concern.

The one who performs his actions with detachment performs on the highest level.

From this space one develops the necessary patience to change.

It is not relaxation or meditation, it is practicing living and playing as your higher self.

The biggest challenge for most people is to not forget this.

Move around the room as if someone else was moving through you. You'll find, if you can imagine it, you instantly glide. Your mind is dormant, at rest, but your body is moving. The actions become pure of all your insecurities, programs, fears . . . all your STUFF.

You sample a moment of perfection that can be lived in all the time. From that space you are graceful, economical, and BRILLIANT.

The beauty and simplicity of this state is too much to maintain, of course, and you'll lose it, but those "flashes" have an effect on your ability to act, your intuition, and even your motor skills.

Eventually you become comfortable with those flashes and realize that you can extend them a few seconds more, or even a few minutes more.

Like plunging into an ocean of nectar and dissolving into that ocean. Playing would cause all limited identification to dissolve. The ego merges with the ocean. You sit there as honored guests while the angels of heaven serenade you with streams of light-filled song.

Theory only has value when it proves freedom.

2 ■ A Bit More History

It started with the wind.

And trees . . . The awakening started while noticing the wind and its effect on the trees. I had always derived some comfort from trees because they shielded me from two repellent forces; sunlight and heat. But now *they were dancing.* The wind made them dance. I never noticed it before but one summer several years ago I spent a lot of time in my backyard watching them dance. How good they were! One set of trees was stage left. They had leaves that were shiny on one side so, when the wind blew, they would change costumes. They were leafy-green, but when the wind blew, they turned around and their costumes were shiny silvery green. They moved back and forth in patterns like a Busby Berkeley production. Center stage was trees with smaller leaves and they were much more active. They went thrashing about when the wind blew. They rushed and taunted towards both sides. Stage right to where I sat were bigger and closer trees. Their large branches featured a lot of smaller branches. The wind made them flap like a mermaid's tale, like gigantic hand fans. These days, when I take walks and the trees dance, I feel like they are talking to me, saying, *"Nice to see you. So glad you're passing by!"* By the way, I don't know the names of those trees, *and I don't care . . .*

I was born with a prodigious talent. Music came so easily to me. When my parents brought in a piano for me to try, I figured out the melodies to any tune I knew and proudly announced, "Good news, Mom, we won't be needing those lessons. I just figured out how to play!" I was also attracted to how popular playing the piano made me. It covered up a host of inadequacies. Although not as athletic as jocks, as smart as nerds, or as tough as greasers, when I played the piano, I was *the man!*

When I was eleven, I had recorded a single and appeared on television shows. I was supposed to be on one of the big late-night talk shows. I was on it, I killed, but when I got home to watch it with my parents, we found that I was cut out of the show. William F. Buckley, the resident conservative in media at that time, had gone on too long so they had to cut me out. (It was then that I became a life-long Democrat!)

We were so disappointed. We called up the show and asked what happened and they told us about the cut but to keep watching the show because they would surely cut it into another night of the show. We watched that show for the next year but I never saw myself on it. I was on the edge of fame but this cruel cut prevented it from happening. Then the show was cancelled. This was important because I think it was right there that I formed a relationship with God, one where he would pull the rug out from under me whenever I was about to receive something I really wanted.

I developed a screw-you attitude at that point, which grew as I got older.

From my teens until my early thirties my main gig was weddings and bar mitzvahs. Every weekend I would put on a tuxedo and play three or four of them. I played a portable organ with some musical cats but was completely ignored or treated as background to the bar mitzvah boy. Again, I railed at God, "Why did you give me this talent and stick me with this shit work?" I began to relish a plan to screw him back. I would take this precious gift he gave me and screw it up completely, waste it, and with any luck, actually kill it off. I worked on this conscientiously from about sixteen until thirty-six years of age. Actually, by about thirty I had yearnings to save my life but it was then I found out that I was addicted to sensually destroying it.

Eventually, I was going to just surrender and make the most of being a wedding musician. If I chose to embrace it, I could make a pretty good living. Playing parties when I was thirteen and walking around with two or three hundred dollars in my pocket was pretty cool. But by thirty years old it had gotten really tired. The same amount of money wasn't that impressive in a thirty-year-old's pocket. I was getting suicidal, doing hallucinogenics and other drugs on these gigs and washing them down with a lot of alcohol. Some of the most bizarre stories of gigs came out of that period, funny stories, but maybe for another book.

My father, bless his heart, realized I was killing myself and told me to stop playing those gigs. He gave me two hundred dollars a week to spend the time at home working on my art, my music, instead of wasting myself every weekend. This went on for a while, but I started to feel like a career as a concert artist wasn't going anywhere. Finally, I decided perhaps I could just surrender to the reality of weekend parties. If I led the groups, called being a sub-leader, I could make a good living. I had a girlfriend from seven years earlier who I had met in Bermuda. After we left there, she came with me to New York but eventually I sent her back home to England. I wasn't ready to settle down because as we say in the business, I hadn't gotten my "shit" together yet. I also wasn't ready to stop partying in New York City, 1970s style. There's a saying about the '70s; if you remember them, you weren't there. Well, I got lost for at least ten years. But then I resolved to quit the dream of making a splash as an artist and go for the American dream, wife, kids, nice house in Westchester, maybe a boat, etc. I was resolved to go to England and ask my long-suffering and long-waiting girlfriend to marry me. I booked a ticket for England and arrived with the great news.

Unbeknownst to me, she had already taken a boyfriend in the town she lived in and never had the heart to tell me. I couldn't blame her; I had packed her off and asked her to wait all these years but I was nevertheless crushed. Not only the heartache of love lost, but the whole plan for the next phase of my life was destroyed. What to do now?

Sometimes the only way to tempt fate is to make a decision. The results may contradict or support the decision, but that's what brings about the results. Sometimes the greatest growth is possible when one's life is sad and one's heart has been broken. At that point one is forced to trust fate. In those moments there is either illumination or despair and nothing in between. So, one must constantly go to the philosophical model and not be lazy. It is a time when you can renounce old habits and forge a new path; an exhilarating time when you can let go of old sorrows. You can welcome each moment connected to your heart. When you're in the illumination you feel no concept of limitations.

I had decided that I was quitting being a concertizing musician and fate, or what I learned later in life was the *Shakti*,[1] had deemed otherwise. I would continue attempting to concertize. Once you make the decision it might or might not be a mistake, but either way it is the right move because you *moved*. More about that later.

I had an open plane ticket. I could go home to my parent's house, crawl into my old bed and weep, or I could use the ticket to go to Western Europe. I had been to England several times to visit my girlfriend, but I had never been to the rest of Europe, France, Germany, Holland, places like that where, in fact, most of the jazz gigs were happening.

I happened to bring a little book with me on the journey titled, *Illusions* by Richard Bach. He was a popular New Age author before the term existed. He had written another more popular book titled, *Jonathan Livingston Seagull. Illusions* had ideas in it that I had never heard. It was the first time it had ever been proposed to me that the problems and dramas of everyday life were more illusion than fact, that how dire the consequences seemed to be was a choice and that I could see a truth beyond that if I were willing. Those ideas have been written to death in the ensuing decades; *The Power of Now,* everything written by Louis Hay, James Redfield, Eckhart Tolle, etc. But at this time in my life, this was completely new and revelatory information. *Illusions* ended the way it started, so if you wanted to you could read it over and

---

1   Shakti, the primordial cosmic energy and represents the dynamic forces
     that are thought to move through the entire universe. The concept or
     personification of divine feminine creative power, sometimes referred to as
     "The Great Divine Mother"

over again. This I did, and in that spirit took a chance and went on to Western Europe.

The first place I went to was Paris. As I was being driven from the airport, I saw the Eiffel Tower and was amazed. I had a mixture of exhilaration, fear and sadness over the loss of my girlfriend, then elation, then back to the book, and so on. I was on a journey, no doubt.

A friend had a friend who worked on a French radio station, and I was invited to record a tape for no reason whatsoever. I played solo piano and sang several songs. Coming out of college I had been a singer as well as a player. I would do Joe Cocker, Beatles, Isaac Hayes, Ray Charles, and a few jazz standards. In taking on this trip, I barely had any footing, so it was nice that someone asked me to do something in this strange new land. I kept reading *Illusions* over and over again to transcend the drama. This book was my rock and my despair was a broken heart. The places in my mind I used for emotional support had crumbled. It was an opportunity to renounce old habits and follow the light towards new pathways and patterns, to let go of old sorrows and move past seemingly solid limitations.

Next, I went to Munich. I had a friend I could stay with there. One night I went to the main jazz club in that town, The Domicile. Brashly, I sat in and got a standing ovation. When I went to the bar a guy said, "You know, I could book you." He was a booking agent evidently.

I had the cassette in my pocket I had just recorded in Paris so I handed it to him and said, "Here, book me."

I also met a girl there and that was a godsend. When you're young and you break up with a lover you think you'll never have sex again. I went home with this girl and I am grateful to her to this day. The next day, I had an appointment to see a couple of record company execs from a very good German jazz label. I played a tape of one of my solo concerts from New York for them. They both laid down and became completely absorbed in the music. When it was over, I had a contract to record my first solo album of my own improvisations. This *trusting the Shakti* business was really starting to work out. A new life was being woven while the ashes of the old life were still smoldering!

From there, I went to Amsterdam to hang with a friend on his boat, which he had docked in one of the canals. It was just beautiful. We jammed and I met new people and I kept rereading *Illusions*. Because I had the courage to take a chance and go on, things in my life were being transformed. By the time I came home, I was over my great love and the career that I had come to the edge of tossing had pulled me back in with a new record deal and a three-week tour in Germany. Now, having broken the ice by going to Western Europe, I got a call that I felt was absolutely related. A friend of mine was playing with the Ron Carter Quartet[2] and, because of visa problems, he couldn't leave the country. He asked if I could sub for him for a European tour in the summer. Now I had two European tours coming! And this one would be first class, big festivals, etc. On the last gig of this tour there was a guy sitting on the far side of the stage just listening. It turned out to be Archie Shepp.[3] He asked for my number and called me shortly after I got home. The result was another *six-week tour* in Europe. I then became a member of his band for the next three years.

So, you see, yanked away from the cliff as I was just about

2   One of the greatest and most important jazz bassists of the century.

3   Great jazz saxophonist, composer, poet, singer and a contemporary of John
     Coltrane.

to jump, I took action, made decisions. You take an action, right or wrong, brilliant stroke or colossal mistake, and it's a success.

During the following years, I was finally playing in concert settings, doing albums and making a name for myself. But there was still some root anger I had with God and why he had given me this talent. Having grown up the way I did, I was so unacquainted with art or culture that I didn't really understand why anyone cared about this music. Traveling in Europe and playing was a revelation in that there was a formidable audience for the complex music we were playing. They actually *cared.* There didn't seem to be too much of that in America at that time. I myself confess to having doubts. Why don't we all put the instruments down and just watch *The Tonight Show?*

I was getting to stretch out and do things that utilized my talent, not enough, mind you, but getting to do some stuff. I still really didn't appreciate it, wondering what the point was, what was the use?

Somewhere along the line I had to deal with my multiple addictions. This is another story entirely. I'll write that story someday but I will have to be buried with a note, "Only to be published after my death." However, when I took that step to get sober, I again made a decision that affected in my life. After being unemployed again for a while, which was a blessing because it allowed me to focus just on sobriety, I started getting offered new and better gigs. Better for my health and better bread, everything. After a few years of sobriety, the resolve started to wear off a bit and I was less motivated to do the things necessary to stay sober. My wife and I had moved out of Brooklyn and away from all the support I was used to having. By now we had a baby girl and

I knew I was losing it. At one point I got on my knees and actually prayed to God. I remember this very well. I said, "God, I am losing my will to hook up a new support system and do what I have to do to stay sober. My recovery is going sideways (which is what it does before heading south!). Please give me a recovery that is *portable*. I swear—that was the word I used—*portable!* It was one of those prayers that I felt deeply and it got answered specifically. A few months later I was invited to play at an ashram in the Catskill Mountains in New York state. While there, I was impressed with the inner knowledge every single person seemed to have, all of which they had received from their guru. The path they followed had an air of freedom, of liberation, compassion, and humility, and they were *happy*. I think the thing I was looking to be liberated from was *me!*

There was a magazine that they published left in my room. The topic that month was creativity. I wondered, was it a plant? No, it just happened to be that month's title. As I read through it, I saw great articles, not only from swamis and the guru, but from ordinary citizens. Great wisdom that frankly, I thought only musicians and artists knew. It was knowledge about how to exercise creativity without fear. But dentists or lawyers were writing these articles! Civilians! How did they know this stuff? It turned out that something I already embodied in my music, joy and freedom, could be attained in one's life and all these people seemed to be on that path. I decided that, although I was a free being in my music, this was to be my university for studying it in my life.

I took one of their intensives. It was three days of great lectures, meditation and chanting. I made the mistake of sitting on the floor when I had the option of sitting in a chair. So, the thing I most came away with was aching hips. But it still felt great to chant and meditate for three days. Upon leaving I thanked them and said I felt really cooled out and maybe I'll do it again someday.

However, when I returned from that intensive, only then did I realize the effect of it. I came home to our beautiful house in New Jersey, with my beautiful wife and daughter and everything had changed. Suddenly I was *grateful* for everyone and everything in my life. Part of my enduring mental disorder was to never see the good in my life, always focusing more on what was wrong than what was right. But suddenly there was my wife doing something at the sink, and I saw a *goddess* standing there! My whole view of life had changed. It was then that I knew this was the path I needed to go on, the one indicated long before by the little book, *Illusions*, had now unfolded and it was clear that I needed to act again.

I left the ashram that day with a picture of the guru, a few tapes, some candles and a book or two to read. You would use the candles and pictures to set up a *puja,* a table with a few items to remember and stare at while the tape of a tamboura was playing. Or I could sing along with one of the chants. So now when I travelled, I could chant and meditate and set up a sacred space in my hotel room wherever I happened to be. In other words, prayers answered, *a portable recovery!*

This provided a golden period that lasted a few years for me. Sobriety, productivity, I chanted every morning, did some yoga and meditated. I found this to be more of a *discovery* than a *recovery* as I had never been here before.

A year later I got involved in the music, playing and recording the chants. One day while I was playing, the guru was in her chair and there were a thousand people in this great crystal hall chanting and becoming intoxicated. I was playing the piano. The guru was occasionally looking at me, infusing me with joy, laughter and enthusiasm. Even . . . gulp . . . *love!* Looking out on these people I suddenly realized, **this is the meaning and the usefulness of my talent:** to be a conduit from a divine source for other seekers who were embodying their own joy and sending light into the world. I was a cog in the wheel, a link in the chain, and if I surrendered my limited thoughts, I would be part of the greatest journey on earth!

My life has been a struggle to realize the easy understanding I have towards music. Many people have it the other way around. They are well adjusted in most phases of their life. By well-adjusted I mean if there's nothing wrong with their life, then there's pretty much nothing wrong. I've had decades where nothing was wrong although it could be better, but nothing wrong, and in my mind *nearly everything was wrong.* This is a very common trait of an addict's brain and I have an addict's brain. But for some reason I was gifted with a lot of wisdom, wisdom that was just there for me, self-evident. It didn't take a lot of work and erudition because if it did, I wouldn't have had it. My daughter was the same way. She'd be on the phone giving advice to her friends who sought her out. She had the gift; pontificating on things she knew nothing about, *and she'd be correct!* I'm about to do a whole lot of that.

This book is very much about the integration of my own journey, as it is about knowledge of the subject. It is because of the confluence of different forces in my being that I am able to now write my second book, *Becoming the Instrument.*

3 ■ The Perfect Instrument

Lord, make me an instrument of your peace . . .

This popular Christian prayer, the St. Francis Prayer, points the way to the ultimate purpose of a human being, not being the doer but *the instrument of the Doer.* Wherever one comes down on who the Doer is, or even if the Doer exists, the fact is, from a philosophical, psychological, religious, spiritual or even scientific perspective, we become more effective, more alive, more grateful, less fearful, more intuitive, creative, improvisational, funnier, more focused, productive, compassionate, peaceful, and more of service—when we *think there is a Doer!*

"Where there is hatred, let me sow love." This action takes work. Sometimes we have to initiate the willingness, "act as if," "fake it till we make it." But if I become the *instrument* of another power, then that conversion may be automatic. The same is true for the rest of it:

Where there is injury, *pardon;*

Where there is doubt, *faith;*

Where there is despair, *hope;*

Where there is darkness, *light;*

Where there is sadness, *joy.*

I find all that to be a tall order. However, I have had the benefit of experiencing the difference between being the doer or the *channel* of the Doer quite clearly by being a musician. *The groove works best when it works alone.* My desire to direct it is the only thing that can get in the way. Or, as I like to say, *perfection already exists, it's people who mess it up!*

Creating the perfect instrument

The Perfect Instrument requires the physical, emotional, neurological, psychological, and spiritual components in a human being to be in alignment. All those elements are compromised by the *world of thoughts.* I will cover these areas here and in later chapters.

In this understanding we accept the idea that we are not the players who play the instrument. *We are the instruments who play the instrument.* To do that we have to reprogram the mind to stay out of the way so we can "receive." We must train the body to execute without conscious thought. We will investigate all the ways the mind interferes with one's true potential. First and foremost, it's the body that plays the instrument. Without self-judgment and other ruses of the ego the body can learn the most efficient ways for a particular body to play a particular instrument. So, what does the mind do? In its proper place, *it enjoys the music, it beholds music, it becomes grateful for the music.* That takes lots of deprogramming and reprogramming. One wants to cultivate a profound acceptance and love of whatever one plays. Full disclosure, musicians can also use this gift to manipulate others. Music history reveals that even a son-of-a-bitch can be the voice of God! Letting the body play and the mind enjoy opens a channel. After all, if criticizing and browbeating ourselves made us play better, we'd all be virtuosos. If you accept what wants to come out, what comes begins to flow.

Accepting what wants to come out also reveals the weaknesses in one's playing more than if one is trying to control the performance. Playing carelessly will really make plain what you know and what you don't know. We will explore that much more in later chapters. But I'd like to whet your appetite with this statement. *One can play all the wrong notes and still be the perfect instrument!*

Leaving the mind (desire) out of the equation, one can program the body to *be* the physical instrument, the one that *plays.* Programming the body to play is more sport than art. Hitting a baseball requires a "quiet" body. Less moving parts. Programming the body requires repetition and patience. Getting the conscious mind out of the way then becomes essential. Impatience, after all, is a tendency of the mind. In allowing the body to adapt we sharpen our tools, our bodies. *We tune our instrument.*

The psychological component of the perfect instrument is a mind empty of desire. The spiritual flavoring might be a mind *full of gratitude.* This keeps one in balance while muscle memory is established in the body. When technique is muscle memory *you don't have to manage technique.* The body performs automatically. So, you can see the different components that make up the instrument—*you*! It also clarifies the subtle differences in the level of performance. The level of one person's playing or another's could be seen as what one does with concentration, the other does automatically. Assessing one's level of technical mastery can then be quantified by how much their body falls short of that goal. In what ways does one have to seek out what to another comes naturally? The perfect instrument is one that embodies precision without management or conscious control. That makes improvising, or "creating and adjusting on the fly" possible. It also differentiates the classical musician's performance from "very good" or even "excellent" to "virtuosic." This explains the many levels of golf, tennis, etc. If one adds the spiritual dimension of *gratitude*, one achieves adjectives such as "miraculous," "revelatory" or "inspiring."

The body as the programmable instrument should open a whole new level of coaching rather than teaching. It only takes one lesson to teach something. Coaching a student until they "own it" takes as long as it takes.

———

What separates the "instrument" from the instrument?
The mind.

The simplest idea of *Effortless Mastery* is that we can live in or act from the conscious mind, or from what I call *The Space*.

Since I wrote *Effortless Mastery* people have often asked me what that means. In the proceeding years of teaching and lecturing I have hit upon the clearest definition, one that I didn't articulate in my first book. ***Effortless Mastery* means the perfect and precise commitment of a complex action**

without thought or effort. In this sense, those of us blessed with normal motor functions *are already effortless masters*. We walk, talk, use eating utensils, write, read, and perform all sorts of amazingly complex actions that no other species is capable of. As I said in the first book, you've used a fork thousands of times. Ever miss your mouth? Some of you can perhaps cite a few times when you were inebriated enough to actually do that. But let's say six times out of 50,000. I'll take that as *effortless mastery*. Asians display similar mastery with chopsticks. People of other origins may have to adapt to that.

Imagine if your execution of playing an instrument, wielding a golf club or any physical act of sport, art or whatever were as natural and *precise* as walking or using a fork? Shoveling snow, which I just did, is a complex action that can be done from muscle memory. But there's a psychological aspect to it as well. One can shovel snow from the mind, i.e., with impatience and resentment. "Shit, this snow is wetter than last night's snow. It's much heavier. Look how much I have left to do," etc. Or they can do it from a sense of being the instrument, *The Space*. One of the most endearing qualities of being an instrument is staying in the moment, which happens naturally from *The Space*. Maintaining an *inner connection*, one shovel full of snow at a time. I once had this experience while vacuuming the rug in my loft in NYC. I started focusing very deeply on each little square inch of the rug, getting down into the fibers in ways I never had before. Eventually I took off the attachment that allowed me to vacuum standing and got on my knees and started scrubbing every little inch of rug. Every once in a while, I looked back on my work and was shocked to see the clear definition of how much territory I had covered, one minute spot at a time. I was literally more patient with each square than I normally would be skimming the entire carpet much more quickly. Because of this detailed work, I was amazed to discover the true color of the carpet! It was a much darker and richer green than I was aware of. It was a watershed moment. Unfortunately, it was over forty years ago and I was on psychedelic drugs at the time. It's taken me this long to realize that if I keep the mind an empty vessel (no expectations) there is no driveway to shovel. There is only *the next shovel full.* Also, if I imagine the mind to be empty (of desire) then the act of shoveling is not me, but my *higher power,* however I define that. *I become the instrument!*

As an improvisor, I watch my hands and imagine they are someone else's hands. I may say to myself, "Oh yeah, this feels great," but after a while I'm not really involved. Or I may stare into space or into the lights from the stage with no consciousness of my hands and it truly feels like someone else is playing. I'm just listening and enjoying what is coming out. As I receive this sound everything develops perfectly, organically and authentically. Many musicians seek to be original, more ego than service. One cannot affect originality, but the true hope and the doable task is to become authentic. *Authenticity is what happens when you're not trying to do anything. Mistakes are only relevant to the conscious mind.*

You hear the same concept from athletes when they get into the zone, or from books like the *Inner Game of Tennis* and all that stuff. From the standpoint of an improvising musician, you become the *witness* rather that the performer. When I give workshops, I describe this state and ask, "Has anyone ever had a gig where you were almost 'watching' yourself play?" Most people say they have. Then I ask, "Weren't you playing really great, the way you've been hoping to?" Again, most respond in the affirmative. "You played so great and inspired on that gig that you still know where you were and who you were playing with, right?" Lots of heads nodding in agreement. Then I ask, "How was the next gig?" Some downturned faces on that one. The next gig is always horrible. I explain why. "You've all had this experience, but it always visits you when you're not expecting it. Most cruelly, it never happens when you *want to show it to someone else!*" I think I spoke of this in my first book, but everyone can relate to throwing darts. Once in a while, you have a premonition a split second before you throw the dart that it's going to hit the bullseye. Everything feels just right and you indeed hit it. Where does the next dart go? You try to repeat the exact relaxation and flow you had from the previous dart but the desire to hit another bullseye makes the toss too precious and the dart heads towards the bullseye but ends up hitting the bottom of the wall. ***Becoming the instrument means programming the perfect motion while programming the mind to be free of desire to hit the bullseye.*** That requires cultivating the great spiritual attribute of *detachment.*

The different components I referred to before can all be practiced separately. They are separate issues but at many points interdependent. For example, as stated before, one could not even cultivate the right level of practice without some degree of self-control, actually, *self-mind-control.* One's practice can lead to having the bullseye experience or the "ultimate gig" experience more reliably.

There are two very important benefits to creating the perfect instrument. Both benefits require a withdrawal from conscious thought. One is physical. Without the mind's desire to become good at something the body is free to take whatever time it needs to really adapt to the act. The other is removing mental patterns and blocks that stand in the way of what wants to happen. We'll be exploring this in several ways.

For example, when I shovel my driveway with the desire to be done with it, I might hurt my back by moving too much snow at too fast a pace. I'm ignoring the messages my body is giving me as to how *it wants* to use the shovel, whereas my mind just wants to get it over with. From *The Space*, or tuning into my body free of my thoughts, my body will use every physical law to its advantage, gravity, leverage, etc. But also, by committing a physical act from *The Space*, one finds that it extends the body's ability, much as how exercise increases one's capacity for exercise. Ironically, it is the one whose mind is unconcerned with how long it will take or where he is in the process that will *allow that process to go forward*. Slow and steady wins the race!

I like to say (not above quoting myself!) "You can never harm yourself playing an instrument. You can only harm yourself *trying to play.*

Once motor skills or muscle memory is established, the act is automatic and we perform on a very high level. The results may vary but the programming of the body does its job. To allow the body the opportunity to learn its most effective way of performing, a whole new way of practicing music must be established. Actually, it is a *very old* way of practicing. A long time ago, students studied with masters, *not people with master's degrees.* It harkens back to an age when we valued the quality of mastery over a quantity of skills pursued.

Creating precision from an effortless place is what the music world calls *virtuosity.* When we hear a virtuoso, we are aware of how great they play but we're not aware of how natural it is for that person to be virtuosic. It must be easy or it wouldn't happen all the time. Mastery doesn't refer to an act done well occasionally or only if one gets enough sleep. The skill or ownership doesn't diminish if one has a cold or is a bit foggy that day. It doesn't refer to something well done two out of five times. It doesn't even mean doing something well five out of five times. *Effortless Mastery* means *the instrument plays itself.* The virtuoso doesn't play the piece. *The piece plays itself while the musician watches, appreciates or dazzles*. He doesn't have to even be jealous of the performer he's observing because *the performer is him!*

One can train squarely towards that trajectory but one has to believe they have the capacity, or at least *not be attached to whether or not they have the capacity. Why not go for it?*

––––––––––

If the musician is the instrument. Who's playing?

That implies that he is the one to be played or played through. For that to take place, the perfect instrument (musician) is not just a perfect motion machine, but also *a perfect thinking machine.* If his body has been programmed to perform, *the mind may be empty of intent,* preferring the sensation of receiving the performance, dancing with intuition or responding with split-second reactions. If one has achieved the awareness of being played, then the question is, **who's playing?** *Ah!* Now, that is the journey of a lifetime! Some may be absolutely sure of who is playing from the outset via their religion or spiritual belief. Or they may embark on a lifetime journey of discovering just who or what that is. They can also decide that The Force will be forever beyond description. Rather than defining it, they will simply and happily *yield to it.* They may allow it to possess them entirely, knowing not where it comes from but having ample evidence that it sure does sound and feel good, *whoever is doing it.* Or it feels so good to just let "the music" do its thing using the player's skills and tools. It's such a relief when, after performing, someone comes up to me and say, "you sucked!" I can then say calmly, "Wasn't me. Don't blame me! Talk to Him." (Pointing upward!)

Instead of playing, *become the vessel through which music is played.* My spiritual pursuit has given names to some of these tendencies. For me, the source is known as "The Self." That's just for me. To be fully connected on the instrument, whether that instrument is the piano, the violin, the paint brush or the golf club, I imagine *The Self* is expressing *"Itself."* By reminding ourselves of the real purpose of all action, we can settle into the "inner chops" that allow the body to find its natural alignment and *become the instrument that plays the instrument.* The energy that courses through me and escapes into the piano is "The Shakti," which I understand to be the Goddess energy that is the personification of all creativity, among other things. It guides the music in my mind and following it is a decision I made a long time before I ever knew the word.

Possession, like brainwashing, has gotten a bad rep. Aren't there things one might want to wash their brain of? Possession can be the ultimate experience if the one possessed finds his talents, endurance, courage, strength, skill, compassion, and creativity expand in ways he could never *conjure from his thoughts.* I guess it depends on who or what possesses you, though in most cases it is the choice of the possessed, morality aside. Western morality has its flaws, as does Western education. It's hard to define where morality ends and control issues of others begin, obscuring true morality. Morality works best as muscle memory and not as a reaction to *fear of consequences in the afterlife.*

One who identifies as the instrument enjoys becoming empty in mind and body, at least empty of unwanted things such as doubts, hopes, desires, strategies, and so on. A body that is empty of desire enjoys a relaxed sort of freedom. It can be as simple as "doing what feels good" or "in the groove." Truly, if you have experienced possession by some force, musical or otherwise, it can be miraculous. It can defy all your previous assumptions about your physical limitations, i.e., warming up, technical exercises, a piano that you're sure doesn't have a forgiving touch, etc.

I've found becoming the instrument in life to be much more daunting, the feeling of non-doer-ship much more difficult to attain. In fairness, the consequences seem much higher in life than in music. I've experienced joy, liberation, peace, and detachment when I play. Why then am I so encumbered in other areas of life? A swami friend of mine once observed, "Kenny, you're such a free being when you're playing the piano. When you're not playing the piano, why don't you just simply stay aware of that?"

I replied, "I've thought of that many times. I've always wanted to do that. The problem is that guy sitting at the piano is really enlightened, but when I get up from the piano bench, *he's still sitting there!*" However, it is possible that experiencing the truth of non-doership in one area may inform other areas. It's on this principle the book has been written. What I've experienced playing music can be applied to any pursuit. These days I do have more moments where I find joy and simplicity in living.

In my music I always become empty at the touch of the instrument. That allows for the possibility of anything to feed me; ideas, love, musical tricks, etc. When I teach the first step on the piano for instance, I have the person sit there and become empty. I call it "going into *The Space*." Then, as they drop their fingers on the piano, if I observe that they've become encumbered in thought, desire or urgency, I say "drop your hands and go back into *The Space*." It means "drop your hands and become empty." It is absolutely necessary training in becoming the instrument.

Anything you practice long enough bears fruit. Whereas my overt spiritual practices have been sketchy and inconsistent, I've had the benefit of practicing detachment at the piano and the blessing of relearning it by teaching it to others for many years. By connecting this solid experience to my darker side, the one who is so attached, I sometimes find it easier to be *the vessel* in other areas. One must detach from all desires if one hopes to become empty. Even a momentary sense of that can work towards a greater conversation. I've had the experience of detaching from my desires and *receiving everything*. For example, I once went to the place where I do spiritual practices. One of the practices is bowing. Bowing to the deities or bowing to the chair of my teacher. This is an act of humility, but I am often not in the right spirit when I do it. Because I have desires, the bow is hampered by ego, excess baggage. This time when bowing I replaced "drop my hands and become empty" with "drop to my knees, bow, and go into *The Space*." It worked.

When one becomes the instrument, the master can play.

One becomes an empty vehicle for the master to play through. Guess what? The experience is available *even if you know nothing about music!* If you put your hands on the keys, let the fingers roam, receive the sound and let it fill you, you can have the highest experience *without even being a pianist!*

There is an old and otherwise forgettable movie called *Green Card* starring Andie McDowell and Gerard Depardieu. She plays an urban horticulturalist who has her eye on a gorgeous apartment but the building board will rent only to a married couple. He plays a waiter from France whose visa is expiring. Out of mutual interest they marry and find out that they have to live together to accomplish both of their aims. The comedy comes from how different they are from each other and how absolutely inappropriate Depardieu is in her life. In one scene she is at an Upper East Side apartment trying to get some "old money" to invest in an atrium. Depardieu shows up because he needs her keys. He is a gruff, vaguely comunist-y type of Frenchman who rolls his own cigarettes and probably doesn't use deodorant. He behaves like a bull in a china shop in this elderly woman's apartment. For example, he starts rolling a cigarette in the dining room and it's obvious no one has smoked in that apartment in many years. He is probably ruining McDowell's chances of obtaining a donation. Then they go to the living room and he sees a piano. He asks if hostess minds if he plays it. He sits down at the piano and starts banging in the most violent, avant-garde way, stringy hair flying like Mozart. This goes on for a while and he ends with one final crash. They show the old woman's face and she has clearly had a life-changing experience because of the random hand-slashing he has done on her piano. No music had ever affected her this way. One hip thing about this moment is that it is totally possible that he was a French, avant-garde musician. There is a great tradition in 20th century Paris avant-garde. He has just given her a violent epiphany, maybe the most profound moment as a listener in her life, *and you don't even know if he can play the piano!*

The word "perfect" may be daunting. We don't mean perfect in the sense of never making a mistake. No, the perfect instrument is one that has learned to keep the ego out of the way and is forever teachable. Having *become the instrument,* we spend the rest of our lives learning to do things, to *tune the instrument.* Part of the unfolding mystery of perfection *is celebrating one's mistakes.*

4 ■ Blocks to *The Space*

Block: *Not Lazy, Overwhelmed! Not staying in the moment.*

As a child, my teachers told me that I wasn't in the room. I would be looking out the window humming to myself. I didn't realize I was humming. That made it marginally cooler, but the big thing was that I couldn't concentrate on what the teacher was saying. I had severe ADHD and Tourette's syndrome before anyone used the terms. I was sometimes sent home from school because of noises I was making; grunts and other weird sounds. It was bad. At home I meant to get right into my homework, but first I had to have some cookies and milk, and then maybe watch a little television. Then I would be ready. Well, the problem was that those two activities didn't make me ready, they knocked me out. From there on it was just the pain of not doing what I knew I should be doing and jiving my parents to get away with it. Neither parent had finished public school and they never believed it was that important. Especially after my musical talent surfaced. Then, no one, not even my teachers, were concerned if I knew a subject or not. They wouldn't fail me in their course because they'd say, "It's all right. We'll see you in Carnegie Hall someday anyway!" This led to so many diseased patterns:

1. Not being able to get any work done,

2. Getting a free pass for a talent that I had nothing to do with,

3. Low self-esteem because even the talent wasn't my doing,

4. Self-hatred because I couldn't or wouldn't do anything,

5. Great fear that someday, someone would find out that I was an imposter!

There are approximately seven years between each child in my family. I once asked my father why that was, and he said, "It seemed every time we moved your mother got pregnant." I was the youngest. Seven years younger than one and thirteen years younger than the other. It was worse than being an only child because I was alone all the time even though I had two brothers. Being teenagers, they had no use for me. I would see them going out the door while I watched television. If you watch *Mad Men;* a show about advertising men in the 1950s and '60s, it illustrates how television grew to dominate the family, increasingly relieving parents and children of the responsibility to engage each other. My brothers grew up in the '40s. By the time I was born, my mother and father were older, increasingly less active and *totally addicted to a TV being on in several rooms all the time.* I don't blame my parents, but they were older and unresponsive, except for my father's obsession with my musical talent. So, most of my programming was a little boy sitting on a couch by himself, watching program after program; the perfect breeding ground for future fear and self-loathing. A faint rallying cry was, "Right after this show, Ma." But there was always another, and another. I'd be on the couch, watching television way too much of the time. When it came time to do my homework, practice the piano, etc., I couldn't do it.

I would be sitting there, swimming in the void and saying to myself, "Get up and go do something. Do your homework, walk outside!" But I would sit there, as if I were immobile, unable to respond, unable to get up off the couch. This is where I became truly dysfunctional. Even in music, when confronted with the prospect of practicing, I was similarly stuck. With every new activity, there was a note of dread. I still reckon with that today. Sometimes it still leaves me plastered to the couch, just like when I was a child.

I can still dread moving from one chore to the next. The block was, and still is, conceiving of the all the things I have to do. As I looked at the stack of school books I brought home, all I wanted to do was procrastinate. My Tourette's would act up and I'd be twitching and making all sorts of noises as I stared helplessly at the pile. Deprograming this has been a life-long quest.

You know, there was a moment I was really proud of as a father. My daughter Katheryn was a lot like me, talented and funny. Thank God she was also like her mother: compassionate, caring about all people and animals, even people that others would disregard. I'd say she had an awesome blend of the two of us.[1]

I believe that I was a normal student until about third grade, but I never knew what happened to disconnect me so abruptly. Katheryn had bad Tourette's as well, and probably

1   Katheryn died in a car crash on October 2, 2006

ADHD. For one thing, she had a mother who really faced these problems head on with doctors and tried a number of natural remedies. Katheryn was creative and very engaged from kindergarten through second grade. Books were still pictures and homework was still drawing, etc. When she came back from her third-grade class, I suddenly saw what happened to her, *and me*. She had a stack of thick books to study. It seemed to go from one level to the other so fast. She sat at the kitchen table, stared at the books almost in tears and acted out with Tourette's sounds and ticks. I was so fortunate to be there! I could help her, something that was never done for me.

I joined her at the table and asked what was upsetting her and, of course, it was *all these books!* A stack of serious looking books. She didn't know where to start, how long she'd have to be there, and the whole thing was overwhelming! I'd like you to remember that word—*overwhelming*. I said to her, "Honey, you don't have to do all this. All we're going to do is pick up the first book and open the first page. And after that, if you've had enough, we'll stop." One book, one page. As we calmly read the page, her Tourette's quieted down. She became absorbed in this one page. When we were done, she didn't want to stop. She wanted to go on to the next page. I believe that my Higher Power put me home instead of on tour; to be home for her and turn it around right there. She became a good and engaged student.

Eventually, she asked us to go to a private school because she was convinced she could learn more there. I was really grateful for that school because they had courses on how to learn, how to study. *God! In my day who ever heard of that?* She became a markedly better student after that. The crisis passed; the problem was solved. By sitting there with her on that fateful night, I found an answer that informs my teaching today and *that I'm still working on myself!*

Do you relate to this? Does your mind buckle under the weight of things you have to get done? Even when focused on one thing, you might lose that focus by thinking about *even the next thing.* I don't have that luxury. If I am not in the moment, it all becomes too much. If I have an assignment or a deadline, I always get it done, but I find when I don't have a deadline I can still be stuck.

I articulated this very well in my first book, which dealt specifically with musicians who wake up *intending* to practice but by the end of the day, they haven't. The block is that they have a number in mind; 2, 4 or 6. These are the number of hours they think they need to practice in order for the practice to be fruitful. (Note: For some reason the number is always divisible by two—I don't know why.) In that case the problem wasn't practicing, but *starting*. Many can relate to this. We are so far out of the moment—out of *The Space*—because by piling up the chores or envisioning the hours needed to do them, *we couldn't even begin.* For this malady, I came up with a five-minute technique. It's a case of "Musician, heal thyself!" I'll quote my other book here:

The 5-Minute Technique

"Here is a little mental trick to get you going. Just tell yourself that *you are only going to practice for five minutes.* Every time you begin, be sure to stop after five minutes, regardless of what's been accomplished. You'll find that if you think, "It's only five minutes," then it will be easy to start. The problem is often not practicing, but starting. Once you've started, you may want to continue, but let your intention be only five minutes. You can always deal with that. Without noticing, five minutes becomes ten, ten becomes twenty, and so on. However, once you start expecting longer periods, *you may stop practicing again!* That feeling of being overwhelmed will return. Always make it five, and consider any more to be a bonus. Five minutes can be most useful indeed. You can reach your goal with surprising efficiency through a series of five-minute practices. You just need a clear idea of what you're going to focus on."[2]

Going into *The Space* in a normal, busy day can be overwhelming. Removing the block is, as they say in recovery programs, *simple, but not easy.* It's simple because all we have to do is come back into the moment. Noticing your breath is the first simple step in transitioning back into the moment. If the body was a clock, the breath would be the second hand. But it's not easy because we're complex creatures and we hold onto our perceived needs. We may be using the suggested technique of noticing the breath going in and out, but fear arises. Sometimes we don't want to go there because we're afraid we'll be doomed to a day of *freedom,* having to live in the moment. *Trapped in heaven with no Wi-Fi!* That's not what we want today. We want *what we want!* One of the biggest blocks to *The Space* is the fact that most of us are walking around in *virtual reality.* You know they talk about virtual reality as if it was a new thing. Humans have always had virtual reality, *between their ears!*

You're walking on the beach in Hawaii, the sun is shining, the ocean is brilliant shade of aqua-blue, walking with your loved one hand in hand, and you're thinking, "Shit, what is my life about really? When am I going to succeed? Am I really that good? I need to practice more. I could probably have been more successful if I didn't have this damn family!"

You see? Virtual reality. (Maybe if I could just watch an hour of TV, I would feel better!)

For this all-too-common tendency, I have something equivalent to the 5-Minute Technique: *the 20-Second Technique.*

The 20-Second Technique

(I may be giving us all undue credit but I think we can do this for *twenty seconds.*)

Stop moving or walking and notice that you are breathing. Keep looking at whatever you're looking at and hearing what you're hearing but look inside, nose pressed at the window of the candy shop, watching the fudge being made. *Watch the breathing store.* Watch how they make breathe—in, breathe—out, etc. You may not want to do this because you're busy obsessing about your life, working things out, that sort of thing. But let that go *for twenty seconds.* (Here's the punch line.) *You can have your neurosis back in twenty seconds!* No pressure to change or to be free, in fact, feel free to return to your obsession-compulsion. *Just take a break for twenty seconds and notice your breath.*

That's it. There's nothing more to it. The reason I invite you to go back to your pain is that if you think the breathing moment will change you, *you won't do it.* Excuses will come to mind like, "Not now. I'm busy" or "I'm not in the right place mentally to do this right now," or I don't want to let go." Guess what? *I hear you!* But you don't have to change. Just give yourself twenty seconds of *the solution,* then feel free to *go right back to the problem!* The problem of being overwhelmed is an old friend, I understand. You're not ready to say goodbye to your old friend, but you can bid him adieu for *twenty seconds, can't you?*

The fact is you can't turn the tide of all those old neurological messages. That would be like turning back a tidal wave. But you can *take a break*. Tell your diseased mind, "I hear you. You're smarter than me. I can't turn you around—but I'm going to *take a break* for 20 seconds, and I'll be right back!" Often, when you return from 20 seconds, the power of what was consuming you has abated, sometimes it disappears for a while. Of course, it will come back, but the 20-second break is *portable* and can be applied whenever you remember to do it and you're willing to do nothing more than that.

It's a David and Goliath deal; you keep throwing stones at you're old, ingrained patterns and—*the giant will fall!* It starts as poking tiny holes of light through the dam, then more holes, larger holes, then the walls of your old pattern become more like Swiss cheese, and continually applied without expectations—*you can actually tear your mind a new one!*

Block: Needing to succeed

How often does our creativity dry up at the precise moment we wish to have it available? Performance of any kind becomes constrained, even though you're more than prepared for your presentation or performance. What makes it suddenly so fragile, whereas it flowed previously? *Needing to succeed. Needing to do well. Wanting everyone to like you and be knocked out by your presentation!* In a sense, the only thing blocking you from having a real impact is *the need to have a real impact!* The need to be admired rarely gets satisfied *because the audience can see the need.* When we lack intrinsic self-respect, we try to derive it by how well we do our work. Ironic, isn't it? The more we desire to be liked or to have our ideas embraced, the more inspiration hides from us. What kind of cruel joke is that? Caring what people think, needing to be a great musician, needing to feel talented—all are taunts of the conscious mind.

As I stated before, I usually start my workshops with musicians by saying, "Think about a time when you really needed to sound good. How did you sound? Not caring what people think, happily being a fool, seeing failure as another kind of success, feeling part of a larger structure that we all serve . . . pretty right-brained stuff if you ask me! Now, I know I'm talking from a complete layperson's knowledge. But in November 2016 we became a fact-free society,[3] so I feel emboldened to continue. We know we all have dark sides. We have things about the way we act that we definitely wish were different. We have small minds when we wish we were nobler. We fear things that we wish we could have embraced and we let opportunities pass us by. There are always times when faith is *trumped* by fear. I know. I've experienced many of them. Then there are also times when we acted and moved as if we were guided. To take a bold action, it helps if you're not daunted by failure. In fact, being able to bless failure is a *form of success!* Indeed, the fool may live his life in the right brain, but being a fool, he doesn't care. Who is more blessed, the one who gets by in this world sweating every move he makes, even if those moves are successful, or the one who

3   The Election

tries things, fails, succeeds, and doesn't lose his enthusiasm?
I obviously think the latter. A musician may be blocked by
having expectations of what he wants to sound like. He will
withhold love of the sound until he hears a sound he likes.
Being in *The Space* is loving the sound *before you make it.*
Drinking in the sound without judgment is very right brain. In
other areas of life, this would mean not withholding love from
yourself until you become the right kind of person. Loving
oneself unconditionally *turns one into the kind of person one
can love.* In business, honoring one's ideas before doubting
them *produces better ideas.* If you ask a musician what he
most wants he might say, "When I play, I really want to sound
good." Sounds reasonable. But let's transpose the issue to conversation. If I ask you, what do you care about when you talk?
You would answer, "Kenny, when I talk to you, I really want
to sound good!" It's easier then to see the shallowness. Do we
want to sound good or do we want to speak about what really
motivates us? The person waiting for the right idea experiences a block. Take writer's block. for example. Writer's block
is staring at a blank page waiting for *the right* thing to write.
Write the wrong thing for a while, the unthinkable, or worse,
the predictable idea, and feel the flow commence.

Indeed, gloriously trotting down the wrong path is a success in itself. One of the wonderful lessons from music is
that this has been how music often progresses. Once I was
leading a retreat. My whole message was about inspiration.
I started playing and a little voice inside said, It's not happening." At that crucial moment I said to myself, Yeah! It's
not happening! Let's go with that! Let's see what that sounds
like! "I plunged into a glorious world of enjoyment.

The christening of The Effortless Mastery Institute (as of

2015) has been all about removing blocks to *The Space*. In my ensemble we work on opening the channels completely, taking up our instruments and "filling the room with sound." It's probably the only class where there is no critique afterward. That would be a violation of the premise. You cannot control and analyze the quality of the music while playing from *The Space*. They don't go together. In order to experience the channel, one has to suspend all judgment. To stay in that space, trust comes into play. "I let go completely, I play my instrument, and fill the room with sound, then I trust that it will all work out." Trust and faith mean it all works out, *even if it doesn't*.

The ability to honor the music that comes through you regardless of what it sounds like ironically leads to a higher level of music. Can you see how this applies to other walks of life? **We need a sanctuary where we can just focus on our state of mind and let the music play itself!**

A success test

Here's another application of this principle. Taking an action can have three results; two of them are successes and one is a failure. Let's say you live in a town where they have one jazz club and you're a jazz musician. There's not much action there but the way one validates themselves is by their ability to get a gig in this club. You want to get a gig there to validate yourself. That's the drama. If you make the call and the club owner says no, your career is over. Of course, all of this is the province of a small, fearful mind.

Here are the three possibilities that might happen:

1. You call, speak to the club owner and say, "I have a great band and I want to play in your joint." The club owner says, yes. Success!

2. You call, speak to the club owner and say, "I have a great band and I want to play in your joint." The club owner says, no. Success!

3. You never call the club because you're afraid he might say no. Failure.

The first two situations are a success and the last is a failure. Why? If you call and get the gig that's obviously a success. If you take the action and don't get the gig that's a success because you took the action. But if you don't call because you're afraid you might not get the gig, that's a failure. Can you see it? One who is not afraid to take action has a 50 percent chance of success for every one of those actions. The more actions taken, the more chance something will work out. Or the failures will aid in making the necessary adjustments to the plan. ***Therefore, anyone who takes action is a success.*** The one who is afraid to act will likely let the best opportunities pass him by for fear of failure.

Other blocks to *The Space*: Negative beliefs

I'm not very talented.

I can't play jazz, I'm a woman.

I can't swing, I'm Danish!

I am not worthy of a _____ career.

(Feel free to fill in the blank for your particular field.)

These are negative beliefs rooted in delusion. Even if they were true, there would be no use in thinking these thoughts. They become self-fulfilling prophecies. If we're to delude ourselves, let's do it with something unrealistically positive:

I AM A MASTER!

Try it out. We'll talk later.

5 ■ Sixteen Variations on "Getting Out of the Way"

Music plays. Your job is to behold the sound.

When ego takes over the music, drop your hands,
detach, and rest in the nectar of your own deep breath.

Play and act from *The Space.* You may make mistakes, but you'll never go wrong.

Get out of the way and find out that there are
no wrong notes, just wrong understandings.

Perfection already exists. It's people who mess it up.

Detach from your own performance and you'll find that music sticks to you like a jealous lover.

Groove is . . . the absence of trying.

When we say "get out of the way" what do we mean?
What exactly is in the way?

*Ego, desire, the desire to play well and to be thought
of as great. Even the desire to make great music.*
These things are "in the way."

The more important you think the work is that you're doing, the harder it is to perform. Dial back to pseudo importance of what you're doing, and notice the flow.

If you're valuing your life by your level of play, that is a sin. After all, it's only music.

Get out of the way and create the way the Creator intended. *Without self judgement!*

My guess is everything was created to be enjoyed and appreciated. My suspicion is, with the free choice we have, we have chosen to complicate it all.

When you view even failure as a success,
there'll be no failure.

Throughout life there's always been "this" and "that."
When "that" becomes "this"...there'll be no "that"!

Perfection doesn't mean you have to be perfect.

Perfection is celebrating one's mistakes.

Quickly they find, there are no mistakes.

If a clock were conscious of itself
it could never keep time.

6 ■ The King's Speech

Did you see the movie *The King's Speech?* It's the perfect example of what can flow when the conscious mind is at least distracted. It exhibits the idea that we play better (using knowledge that's been sufficiently digested) when we *don't think about it.*

The story is about Prince Albert, who would later become King George VI of England (played by Colin Firth). He was unexpectedly pressed into duty when his brother, King Edward VIII, abdicated the throne in order to marry an American divorcee that he had fallen madly in love with. The nightmare for Albert was that he had a horrible stutter and could not make it through public speeches. Having the crown thrust upon him would be humiliating for himself and for England.

Speech therapists of the day treated the impediment as if it were only physical, but one very unconventional therapist had a different theory. Lionel Logue (Geoffrey Rush) believed it came from deeper psychological issues, a strange notion at the time.

The part I wish to highlight here is early in the film. Prince Albert's first meeting with Lionel infuriates the royal, but he has him perform one experiment. Logue had a new-fangled invention; a record recorder called a Silvertone. He put headphones on the prince and played *The Overture to La Nozze di Figaro* by Mozart very loudly. Then he gave him the famous soliloquy from Hamlet, "To be, or not to be . . ." We don't hear the prince speaking. We only hear the orchestra. Albert, frustrated by Lionel's "method," rips off the headphones and choses to leave, saying that this was not for him. Lionel tells him to at least take the recording home as a souvenir. After another disastrous speaking engagement, the prince, sitting at home, decides to put the recording on and hears himself speaking as never before, "To be or not to be, that is the question . . ." He speaks the soliloquy until he stopped without a single stutter! He realized that this unconventional therapist had the answer for him and their interaction is followed for the rest of the movie. That is an example of distracting one's self from the conscious mind. His stutter *disappeared when he focused on something else.* I've taught students with everything from a physical impediment to a mental block of some kind. Interestingly, it also applies to musicians that already play great, but fill their heads with the *conviction that they don't.* In all cases, when I pulled their attention off of the performance, they flourished.

It recalls another fantastic story I was told about Art Tatum.[1] The story goes like this: Tatum was recording a solo piano album. His greatest devotee, Oscar Peterson,[2] came to watch the session. Sitting in the recording booth, he noticed Art playing with headphones on. This was strange because headphones are used in the studio so that the musi-

---

1   A great jazz pianist, in fact possibly the greatest pianist of all time.
2   Also, one of the all-time greats.

cians can hear each other when isolated in separate rooms. But Art was playing solo, no need of headphones. Oscar asked the engineer why he was wearing headphones. The engineer replied, "He's listening to the World Series!"

Incredible! Tatum's flow was probably all the greater for not concentrating on the playing. His hands already knew what to do. It's not magic. If one has mastered the technique, not only can the hands play by themselves, but are probably better served *if one stays out of the way!*

I know this to be true. It's not a theory or just a good story. It's my reality. In the good old days, before the Internet or even cable TV, the World Series was on plain old broadcast TV. We had TVs that had the equivalent portability of modern-day laptops, I guess, except batteries were not available. You needed to plug it into the wall. I remember playing a duet concert. The grand piano was open, facing the audience of course, leaving a lot of hidden space behind it. I set up my portable TV, watched the game for the whole concert and didn't stop once. Without my control, the ideas just kept coming, unfolding as organically as in nature. I was dimly aware that the music was beautiful but my mind was lightly monitoring the game.

Many years ago, I was playing a gig at Fat Tuesdays in New York City. That club had a horribly dry sound on the bandstand. It had a low ceiling and a mirror for a back wall. For whatever acoustic reason, I always had trouble playing there, trouble getting in the groove. One of those nights I was struggling just to groove on the tune when I looked at the wall to my left. That was the mirror. As I watched my *hands play*, suddenly I started grooving like a (insert profanity here). Then I looked away and again I struggled. I looked back at the mirror again and my hands again fell in the groove. In other words, while I watched *his hands play*, they grooved. When they became my hands again, I struggled. It provided another piece of the puzzle for me.

Another example was more recently, while recording my most recent (as of this writing) solo piano album titled, "The Space," I tried the Art Tatum idea. For the first thirty-five minutes of that recording, I listened to a talk. I wasn't paying attention to my hands. What came out was not on the virtuosic level of Tatum, because that technique simply isn't there, but it was the most organic, flowing and evolving sequence of music I could have ever played. It's why I named the album, "The Space." Finally, I had recorded something that was completely from *The Space!*

There are less dramatic ways of diverting one's attention for the greater flow. Many musicians do it but they hadn't thought of it in this way. Ask successful jazz musicians what they're focusing on and they may say they just focus on the drummer, or the soloist. They're actually doing the same thing. By focusing on the soloist, they've taken their attention off of every little thing they're doing. The result, by the way, is an uncanny coalescence of the entire group, true symbiosis. The Miles Davis bands were most famous for having a chemistry that even dwarfed the virtuosity of the individual members. I dare say that if classical musicians become similarly acquainted with that part of their brains the orchestra would be transcendent!

Just what this is and how and why it works is the subject of a number of the following chapters. Two recurring themes in this book are witnessing but not being ensnared by the conscious mind or thoughts, and training the body so that *it plays*. In that spirit, I always like to say, *my mind is smarter than me and my hands play better than I do.*

7 ■ Meditation #1

"True union is only a breath away."

or

**"True union, true union, I seek you, true union,
you're only a breath away!"**

(Sung to the tune of *Tomorrow*)[1]

*Go to **Kennywerner.com/downloads** and get Kenny's
new meditation tracks.*

Begin by noticing you are breathing. Let's do the simple exercise mentioned in chapters five and six. I'm not saying to follow your breath, but just notice *that you are breathing*. As I said, it's as if you were sitting by a window and there was traffic on the street below and I asked you to watch it. It's that simple. Nothing special going on here. You are breathing in and then breathing out. Just notice that. As you notice you're breathing, you're not thinking. As I said before, if you notice you're breathing, you're not thinking, and if you

1   Recording of the spoken word and music will be available.

have a single thought, at that moment you're not noticing your breathing. So, no matter how many times you have a thought, just catch that and say to yourself, "thought," and go back to watching the traffic out the window. Go back to noticing your breathing. You can do this many times a day. For even a few seconds. You could be filled with angst, or thoughts of things that must go your way, thoughts of things you have to do or people you must persuade, and at any moment you can stop . . . and just notice that you are breathing! Play with that for a minute or two and enjoy the music. Hear the music but don't listen.

Imagine you're an empty shell, completely empty. Nothing is going on inside. The shell has no will or desire, but the shell moves. Imagine your shell being filled with an exquisite nectar. You are just watching, vacant somehow, not participating. Feel the shell filling with the delicious nectar, filling your feet, ankles, up the calves, knees, thighs, buttocks, and hips. Now, feel the nectar fill your stomach and chest, filling your shoulders, and now flowing down your upper arms, elbows, forearms, wrists, hands and fingers. Feel the nectar fill your fingers like pouring water into a glove. Now feel it rising up your neck, into the back of your head and filling your head, cheeks, eyes, forehead, and ears. Feel the top of your head get damp from this nectar and it is the most exquisite feeling. While all this is happening, you are still just sensing that you are breathing, but now it feels like breathing under water. Your shell is now only outer skin, like a water balloon filled with nothing but exquisite nectar. I imagine the syrup they pack canned peaches in, sweet, syrupy goo but tasting heavenly. You might imagine it to be milk or cream that fills the moon and makes it white. Whatever feels good.

Now imagine that your skin is stretched wonderfully as you are completely filled with this liquid. Imagine it is liquid energy. Now, imagine it's *just* energy. You are now like a helium balloon, lighter than air. You don't move, you don't think, you don't *do* anything. You just . . . breathe.

Imagine a higher force—God, if you like—moving your arms. Imagine your eyes are lenses for this Higher Being to look through. All actions are God's, using your body. You are there, but you're just an observer. The Higher Force has taken everything over. You are just a conscious shell, conscious of what's happening but not involved in any way.

What if you don't believe in God; what if there is no God? You could use any force that you were convinced exists, and surrender to that force. Nature, the super-conscious mind, the right side of the brain, Bruno Mars, or whomever you imagine.

Now move from this empty place. Or rather, let that power move through you. Keep watching and don't get in the way. Imagine you're having one of your most productive, creative days, and *you're not doing anything.* As soon as you're conscious of doing, stop, realign yourself with the breath, and return to *not doing.*

———

Now, listen:

In life there are unexpected turns. Actions taken freely are liberating. You feel like you're not doing. It's a feeling of following and trusting. When you imagine the empty shell filled with a Supreme Presence, it's the performance of your dreams. Let's start again. Stop thinking, stop seeing, stop doing, stop caring, stop wishing, stop worrying. But be an empty shell . . . divert your attention towards your breath.

This time, imagine you are a statue, very still. But there is one flexible part, bellows in the middle of the chest. It feels elastic as it expands and contracts. It expands when filled with air and contracts when it expires, naturally. Now focus on that one elastic muscle in the middle of the chest. Like mini waves rushing in and receding, it moves with a pendulum-like steadiness. Now, for a moment, imagine an empty space, an empty warehouse that hasn't been used for many years. Quiet, vacant. But there's a clock in the warehouse that has continued to work. Tick-tock, tick tock; it's the only sound in the room, the only motion in the stillness.

Coming back to the body, you sit comfortably in the space of the empty shell and become hypnotized by the elastic muscle inflating and deflating . . . like the tick tock of the clock. Let its pendulum motion hypnotize you, or become lost in the feeling of expansion and contraction. Use your imagination. Or just pretend. We pretended when we were children. When did we lose that?

There is an old proverb. *Do nothing and nothing shall be left undone.*

Just imagine, you're not doing anything. It's being done while you watch.

———————

Effortless Mastery means playing from the heart, playing from your true self. Very few learn to do that. Not just playing from the heart, but receiving the music the heart gives. Become empty of desire now and let the heart play.

The first step . . . The first step . . .

8 ■ A Commercial Break
THE MIND!

I want to be a tree. Consider the tree. Lots to learn there. How blessed they are not to have a human mind! A tree stands there, rooted to the ground. It endures rain storms, ice, and extreme cold or hot weather. But it never wavers from its duty, which is to provide oxygen, coolness and shade. Even if lightening were to strike it dead, it would quietly accept its fate. Then it would give up its body and create mulch and nutrients into the ground. Perhaps it would be fodder for a whole forest. A tree does its duty. It's not bothered by a sense of them and us. No, that's the dubious province of the human mind. The human mind has tremendous potential to create. But along with "great freedom" comes "great side effects."

What separates us from the moment and from each other? *Thoughts.* Trees feel as one, so do birds, why not humans? Because humans have an extra gift—and curse—the power of thought. It may well be that other living organisms think, trees included, but it's a much less complex mental landscape. Doubts, fears, low self-esteem, pride, embarrassment, insecurity, needing to sound good on a musical instrument, all of the obstacles to a simple existence reside in our minds. *I don't believe a tree lacks confidence.* One travels to the Himalayas to meditate to achieve the possibility of not thinking, *just being.* When one has experienced that, all prayers have been answered. But by the time he has returned to Bhuntar Airport—poof!—it may be gone.

You know, when God made the mind, he should have made a TV commercial like the pharmaceutical companies. The commercial first tells you what the medication does and the rest of the commercial is warnings of potential side effects.

It might go something like this:

There's a guy, presumingly a family man, opening his garage door with a big smile on his face. It's a sunny day and everything is fine. The voice-over says:

The mind! A wonderful new product from God to man, his latest creation. With a mind you can appreciate God's work. Only with the mind can you construct a world of your own and do what no other animal can do: Think! Create! Love! Appreciate! Worship!

Up to this point a big smile on the actor's face, taking deep breaths and enjoying his surroundings.

Then the voice says:

Potential side effects: Fear, rage, anxiety and anger, resentment, envy, discontent, insecurity, constant hunger for sensations, selfishness, urge to conquer and control, not loving yourself, comparing yourself to others, and extreme vanity.

While this is being read, his face suddenly turns dark and paranoid. He looks suspiciously from side to side; beads of sweat appear as he struggles with anxiety.

But in the next shot he's hitting a baseball to his son or pushing his granddaughter on a tire swing as these words scroll down the screen.

The voice narrates:

A mind may not be right for everyone.

Stop using if:

> *you hate yourself,*
>
> *can't forgive yourself or another,*
>
> *find yourself ungrateful for what you have and don't have,*
>
> *jealous of others,*
>
> *use substances to drown out thoughts,*
>
> *sabotage yourself with fear or resentment.*

More side effects include:

> *the urge to gamble,*
>
> *sex addiction,*
>
> *suicidal thoughts.*

If you experience any of these symptoms contact a licensed therapist or local pastor immediately.

If you have any of these side effects for more than twenty years, please see a licensed psychopharmacologist.

And now it's back to our movie . . .

**In the mind bondage,
in the mind liberation.**
/ Ancient Sanskrit saying /

!

9 ■ Left-Brain/ Right-Brain Integration? Why, Yes!

Another way to look at things is through a bit of pop science:

RIGHT HEMISPHERE
Function: Responsible for control of the left side of the body, it is the more artistic and creative side of the brain.

LEFT HEMISPHERE
Function: Responsible for control of the right side of the body, it is the more academic and logical side of the brain.

I have always preached, "Practice and acquire knowledge from your left brain, play from the right brain." In my musical life, I slip into my right brain very easily. Playing and performing is, for me, totally right-brained. What does that mean? It's *don't-sweat-the-small-stuff* kind of thinking. It's a question of what one views as *the small stuff.*

From the left brain, one worries if everything is all right. From the right brain, one views everything as perfect. Of course, on the face of it, that's very impractical. But triumphs happen from a right-brain state of mind that can't come any other way, whether it be in business, war, or art. A great artist knows it. The right brain is where creativity, inspiration and invention lie, where risks are taken. But there is a lot of left-brain also involved. A lot of methodical thinking can work in support of an idea from the right brain. These are ideas the conscious mind acknowledges but can't really depend on. *We think of them as "too good to be true."*

The left-brain is a very good place to acquire the skills that will support the flow, but not the best place for the flow to happen. In music, that's called *performance*, groove, and acceptance. No matter what style of music one plays or what technique it demands, in performance there is no time to quantify or judge, only to appreciate and admire. There is no time to look, only to find. The more appreciation, even gratitude, one has for that flow, the more it flows.

Practicing, as I said, is best done from the left-brain. I have told my students that if you find your practicing to be very inspiring, you should be suspicious. You might not be getting anything done. Practicing is practicing and playing is playing, and the twains shouldn't meet too much, or so I proselytize. This is an important principle to absorb. The joy of playing is liberation and the joy of practicing is concentration. Right-brain, left brain. But actually, there is a subtle crossover. From the left-brain one is concentrating, and from the right-brain one finds oneself absorbed. It is so common for students of all skills levels to practice and not improve. One of the main reasons is that they are being creative when they really need to build language.

The opposite is not great either. Many find themselves practicing, looking for language, while in performance. *That can really gum up the works!*

But who is to say that the right-brain is only for dreaming and being an artist? While in my creative space, I have envisioned systems that are innovative for accomplishing left-brain tasks, for example, building piano technique. If one spends time forging a deeper connection to the right-brain, even thinking from their right-brain, seemingly impossible or unforeseen connections may appear. But those right-brained moments, or epiphanies, are totally informed by left-brain knowledge. I think of that as left-brain/right-brain integration. The integration is important because many people are short on one or the other. Solely left-brainers can't dream, and right-brainers can't practice and prepare. They don't learn too easily either. As an old friend of mine once said, "The bars are full of talented people."

I invented a composing process I call, "random composition." It perfectly illustrates the point of this chapter. From my flow state, I found a versatile way of building and expanding musical compositional sequences. It accomplishes what left-brain systems crawl toward in the study of music theory. The crucial element is a state of detachment, letting the mind and the composition drift aimlessly. It's in the *"how'd-you-come-up-with-that?"* category. One generates notes from the right brain, even enjoying chaos, then removes things until a system appears, walking back chaos until form appears. In the recording studio I have experimented with the band turning off their headphones. I have to tell you, for better or worse, that's the most stimulating music I've ever heard! Their right-brained (maybe hair-brained!) ideas moved the music to really far out places. At least, I thought so.

And that's the point. Most every innovation has been made by people who rose above left-brain concerns. Sometimes it works, sometimes it doesn't. That's the price you pay to play. So even when doing left-brained activities, maybe it makes sense to access the right brain for a bit. That could be breathing and gazing out to nowhere.

Imagine really creative ideas that create radical new pathways, much more powerful than previously known. There's so much left-brain information involved: the use of technology, everything that has been previously studied, and mastery of all or most previous paths. But what forges the new pathway? The pathway is forged by the ability to create, the ability to dream, perhaps extreme nonsense until it makes sense, a comfortable relationship to failure; in other words, properties of the right brain.

Characteristics of this type of thinking are editing without attachment, and allowing the composition to grow and material to build without breaking in and asking, *"What is the meaning of this?"* I like not to be stuck in any kind of process and allow it to come from wherever it wants to. Sometimes, I write the most predictable, most heartfelt, sappiest melodic song. That's what wants to come and I let it. I don't left-brain it with thoughts like "This is too predictable." I could see the opposite being true for many. *"My music is this or that."* One can break out of boxes by randomly writing nonsense and just allow it to flow. Writing nonsense is very right-brained, but the ability to write notes is acquired through the left. The right brain says to follow your passion! Follow your whimsy! Follow your soul or genitals—whatever speaks to you.

When I teach people to go into *The Space,* I am inviting them to enter the doorway of the right brain. We slowly learn to move and do things from there. That means integrating left-brain activities into the right brain, like writing or speaking. Allowing those faculties to be controlled by the right brain is to risk being the fool. The left brain is for definition. One must be able to distinguish, quantify, and move from one activity to another with a fair amount of competency. But work may flow easier when one commits those acts with detachment or while "witnessing" oneself.

Getting out of the way is right brain. Therefore, the new mantra for me is not "practice from your left brain, play from your right," but "left-brain/right-brain integration." Even breathing between left-brain tasks would invite the integration I have described. In my case, if I let the right brain take over, I may rise like a phoenix from the couch and apply myself. From the left brain I might think, "Gosh, I've got so many things to do, I don't know where to start," hence, being forced back to the couch. From the right brain, I think of one thing and can get on with it. Even having faith is very right brained. It's not easy to reason oneself towards faith. That's why they call it "a leap of faith." (Leap over the left and enter the right!)

Science is discovering more and more about the functioning of the brain, and how it responds to different stimuli. I'll leave it to the reader to investigate the science, which is well documented. When one is mired in addiction, a certain part of their brain lights up. When one prays, it illuminates a different part of the brain. That part promotes a feeling of well-being, faith in the Almighty, love, compassion—all the good things one hopes for. It feels as if God has, in fact, answered our prayers. That may or may not be the case. This discovery doesn't prove or disprove the existence of God. But it certainly proves the *power of faith*. Faith moves one from the fear of the mind to the space of the heart. That's the right brain.

The musical equivalent of enlightenment is this statement: *Every note I play is the most beautiful sound I've ever heard.* One who believes this is dwelling in the state of non-dualistic reality of the Upanishads, Avaita Vedanta, Buddhism and even Christian Mysticism. In the King James version of the English Bible the text reads: *"The light of the body is the eye; if therefore thine eye be single, thy whole body shall be full of light."* Though it's practiced in life by the highest dedicated ascetics, applying it to music would be considered heresy. This biblical passage can be converted to, "If thine eye be single, every note shall be full of light."

The virtues of Individual Mind and Universal Mind will be discussed in the next chapter. I can tell you that non-dualistically speaking, *all sounds are full of light.* What part of the brain lights up when we're afraid life could all go off the rails? What part of our brain is lit when we embrace success or failure with equanimity, when we *trust ourselves?* This is how inventors have the stamina to go forward. They are absorbed in a process and not daunted by the dualism of success or failure. Great composers, too!

What is not commonly understood is that one can do mundane tasks while supported by the power of faith, or by right-brain activity. Boredom may turn into connection. Ordinary moments become extraordinary. But one may be hampered to perform even simple tasks by a mind that won't quit. Doubt, fear, and extraneous thoughts pervade one's conscious awareness while one is simply trying to get through the day. If one surrenders those thoughts to a larger force, they may perform their left-brain activities on a magic carpet of flow, a jet-stream of faith that they are in the right place at the right time. They may feel unburdened and free to live their life. The activity might be left brained, but performed from the right—the *real connection.* Ego promulgates the perception of separateness, which is more commonly understood.

I have been to spiritual locations where people perform left-brain functions, like cleaning a toilet or polishing a railing. Connected to the "God" part of their brains, I've seen the most angelic looks on their faces. A seemingly meaningless task done with such love—the ordinary transformed into the extraordinary!

As stated before, when I teach the first step towards that goal, I teach how to "go into *The Space";* in other words, to become empty. We even empty ourselves of what we think is and isn't important. We do this before we touch the instrument. We may do it in several ways. The first way is to simply follow the breath: Follow the in-breath and out-breath. Don't exaggerate; just observe it going in and out. Sometimes I guide by asking them to stare at a spot on the wall. We might stare so hard we could bore a hole in the wall—X-ray vision like Superman. This has the effect of taking one away from being the subject to being the observer. In that case, where do they go? Essentially, it is a migration from self-conscious thoughts to the right-brain domain of being aware from an expanded place. Whereas the self-conscious state is so constricted with lies or dangers not "clear and present" in that moment, the right brain soars above the ruins and allows a left-brain activity to flow.

I will ask the student to invest all their focus in a spot on the wall or perhaps look at the ceiling. This technique leaves the player no alternative but to "trust the hands."

There are some who are so used to controlling their hands that they can't really give up control, so we settle for distraction. I may ask them to follow my hand with their eyes wherever it goes. It could be over their head or on the floor by their feet or I could move quickly back and forth.

The point is, in order to follow my hand, they have to follow my hand. While engaged, I'll say without warning, "play a note." The result is the most organic playing of the note. Sometimes I do funny things, like having them count backwards from 100 or 1,000. If they are from foreign countries, I'll ask them to do it in their native tongue. Sometimes I'll count and tell them to pay attention to my counting and I'll go, "1, 2, 3, . . . 58, 57, 4, etc." Since they don't know what number is coming next, they are forced to pay attention. Sometimes I'll say to them: "Where are you from? What are your parents' names? Your brothers and sisters, what are their names and ages?" I have them do this while their hands are on the piano. They're answering me from the left brain, and playing the instrument from the right. It forces them to give up intellectual control.

This dialogue distracts them from caring, which ironically, is what's holding them back. Distraction isn't as good as becoming empty. In becoming empty, there is the possibility of entering a union with greater forces. But at least distraction releases the tight grip of the conscious mind. *"I'll let go of my self-obsession when you pry it from my cold dead hands!"* Paradoxically, it creates the true connection. The object is to remain in *The Space* while the body moves. (Or at least keep watching Netflix while the body moves.)

I asked a very good friend and adviser of mine, Bradley Horowitz, to tell me if left-right brain integration occurs in the tech field and if so, how? He has a sterling resume as an entrepreneur, programmer, inventor, and innovator. Horowitz was a major exec at Google, spearheading Google+. Much more can be said about Bradley Horowitz. (Google him!)

The following is what he said and a brilliant example of what this chapter is about.

"What's interesting is when you take on a project, a lot of it is sort of like architecture. You have a blank sheet of paper in front of you and you know you want the correct outcome. For the correctness of any computer program, you have a given set of inputs and an expected set of outputs. But what happens to turn that input into the correct output is a creative process. No two programmers, no two teams, no two companies will do that the same. That's what's fascinating: On the one hand, you're talking about the most rigid, left-brained, sort of rules-based structure.

"The computer is completely unforgiving. If you leave a semi-colon off, it won't work. And yet, no two programmers will build things in the same exact way and there are huge variations in the creativity and the expression of how one would do that."

––––––––––

He goes on. "Similar to music or athletics or any creative endeavor, there's this flow, or this 'zone' (*The Space*) that you can get into, which is amazing. For me, a lot of it has to do with zooming up and down across the various levels, sort of the grand overview of what you're trying to get done. And then there's the thought, 'I know I'm going to need this at some point.' So, I'll start writing this little thing and that little tool that you build for yourself. Now that you have that tool, you build something 'meta' that sort of works with that tool. You're constantly moving up and down from the blue-print of what you're trying to build down into the minutiae of executing the sub-routines and code that is actually doing the work.

"This flow is why sometimes programmers will go for 12, 14, 15 hours straight *(it does sound quite addictive!)* because, when you're in the zone you're holding so much context in your head that you don't want to lose it. If you do have to get up for a 'bio break' *(new terminology for me!),* it's still in your head. Wherever you're going, you're carrying all that with you.

"Eventually, you do reach a point of diminishing returns. You're falling asleep on your keyboard, starting to make mistakes, or whatever. Then you put it all away *(drop your hands),* you go home to sleep and somehow the brain, in this magical way, awakens you with this 'eureka moment,' and you see how it all fits together or how the problem can be solved in a more elegant way. *(This is so similar to com-posing for me or even the writing of this book!)* But that's not a striving process. That's a flash! That's the 'muse' working through you." *(That's the right brain.)*

"I think anyone who has seriously programmed or *pas-sionately* programmed in this way has had the experience of getting into the flow, of surrendering to the process of reaching a point of diminishing returns, stepping away, and allow something to come to you that isn't striving."

Here, I strayed off the topic of this chapter. I told him that a basic move in *Effortless Mastery* is dropping your hands between repetitions. I posed this question to him: "You know how one's hands remain on the keyboard while one is thinking? What might happen to the resilience of the mind if programmers dropped their hands when not typing?

Don't they usually keep their hands on the keyboard, much like pianists?"

He thought it was an interesting and unexplored idea. He said, "I'll tell you, if you look at the posture of most computer programmers, it's as bad as you would imagine. These are people who are not in touch with the physicality of their bodies. Almost like 'brains in a jar.' I think there might be an opportunity to explore what role the body and the breath might play—"

————

I interrupted. "While doing the work!"

He said he didn't think anyone had brought that up yet.

What about issues of courage and fear? For one who's not afraid, where does that fortification come from? A soldier is moving intuitively—from the right brain, but trained for the mission from the left. The battle becomes the reality of the moment. Amazingly, this is the creative brain, the improviser who is not attached to previous realities. I am reminded of Tom Hanks' character in *Saving Private Ryan*.[1] Hanks plays Captain John H. Miller. Before the war, Miller had been an English composition teacher since 1933, was married, and coached the local baseball team. I think a subplot of the movie is this man's evolution. Coming from a normal civilized existence, he had only one simple goal when he left to fight World War II: to return home to his wife. But on the battlefield, he performed with heroism, and his total devotion to the mission probably expanded his courage to a level he didn't know he had. Left-brain baseline giving way to right-brain action? Perhaps that's how it works.

1   https://savingprivateryan.fandom.com/wiki/John_H._Miller

An important subtext of this book is that the right-brain activity can be practiced so that it becomes more available in the moment. If faith, surrender, and detachment can be practiced, perhaps courage can, too.

From my own experience in the right brain, every note is the perfect note. Every mistake is a gift, and my level of success is irrelevant to my own state of self-love. One will learn to trust this state because more often than not, they'll create something that couldn't have happened any other way. Big minds make big mistakes! The mastery of language is left brain. If I own that language, then it is the right brain that speaks. If I can infuse left-brain tasks with right-brain flow, then I'm going to write four books a year and two symphonies a month. Well, maybe not, but imagine not needing to write a good symphony. One could fill page after page! Left-brain/right-brain integration may allow one to become the instrument.

The answer may be like an Uber driver at the airport, parked and waiting for you in the right brain.

10 ■ A Broader Interpretation: Individual Mind/Universal Mind

The concept of left brain/right brain can be expanded to the concept of *Individual Mind/Universal Mind.* Left brain corresponds to the individual mind. As stated previously, it's a very useful part of our makeup, allowing us to get to work on time, wear matching socks, and make sure to get paid on the gig, etc. It is essential in the acquisition and storing of knowledge. However, individual mind is also the part of us that obsesses, worries, fears, resents, and is generally more aware of our individual selves.

Properties of the right brain expand to what has been labeled in ancient spiritual and philosophical texts as Universal Mind. From the perspective of this book, when one acts while attuned to Universal Mind, *one becomes The Instrument.* It is what I came to refer to as *The Space.* An attribute of Universal Consciousness is feeling part of the greater whole, incurring the power of Supreme Energy, Supreme Bliss—a current too strong to be short-circuited by the individual mind, i.e., *thoughts*.

————————

The nature of the Universal Mind is:

Omniscience (all-knowing),

Omnipotence (all-powerful),

Omnificence (all-creative), and

Omnipresence (always present).

All these qualities are present within us.

We can quote many great beings to illuminate this concept:

"Everything is energy."
and

A human being is a part of the whole, called by us the Universe. / Albert Einstein /

You don't have a soul. You are a soul. You have a body. / Generally attributed to C.S. Lewis /

The universal soul is the alone creator of the useful and the beautiful, therefore to make anything useful or beautiful, the individual must be submitted to the universal mind.
/ Ralph Waldo Emerson /
(The most useful quote for the artist!)

I am everywhere. / Bhagavan Nityananda /

The Universal Mind goes by many names: Superconscious Mind, Universal Consciousness, God and his many names—Brahman, Jehovah, Allah, etc. I postulate that you can give it any name and still connect with "It." I'm with Francis Bacon when he said, "I had rather believe all the fables in Legend, and the Talmud, and the Alcoran (Koran), than that this universal frame is without a mind."

Properties of individual mind

Feeling alone and unsupported, the "weight of the world on one's shoulders,"

Being in a contracted state, vulnerable to mental activity,

Fears arising,

Attaching too much importance to unimportant issues,

Being known as "small minded,"

Having boring, mundane thoughts, and

Defining self by level of achievement.

Properties of universal mind

Its nature is love, light, and incomparable bliss,

one with your Higher Power,

Watching the good, the bad, and the ugly come and go with relative equanimity,

Higher Power experiences "The Self." In this sense, we can be the eyes and ears of God.

We become the voice through which "It" speaks to others, i.e., the highest principle of music,

The Supreme permeates our thoughts,

Inner expansion to this force, whether real or imagined, and

Living in the bliss of freedom, free of self-imposed restrictions.

By now, you know when I say "conscious mind" I mean the part of our brain that thinks. After all, if you weren't thinking, you wouldn't be aware of your mind at all. Thoughts are evidence that you have a mind, not just a brain. All animals have brains, but no other living organisms can think in such detail as we can.

After I take my dog out in the morning and give her a biscuit, I sit in my living room to meditate while the coffee is percolating. My dog is the most affectionate, sweetest dog you've ever met. She always wants to lie next to you on whatever piece of furniture you're on. After she's gotten her treat, she sits in front of me for a moment. She looks at me, then looks up the stairs. She's trying to decide if she should get up on the couch with me, or take advantage of the fact that I have vacated the bed and take my place next to my wife. I can see her thinking about it and I am always amused, so there is at least that level of thought. But I have the power to observe her thought process.

We can all agree that humans have thought and compu-tation power far beyond any other species. But for all we are aware of, there is an infinite amount of energy and power that we are not aware of. It is a part we could never entirely understand because that power is infinite and the part of us that thinks is finite.

In the movie, *What the Bleep Do We Know?*, Dr. Fred Alan

Wolf makes a statement that has become a tenet of my own spiritual understanding: "Asking anyone to explain time is like asking the fish that is swimming in water, and only knows the water, never has been out of water, never been hooked by a fisherman or something like that, to explain water, to know that it's in water." That makes impeccable sense to me. I like what I've said for years in misquoting Dr. Wolf: "Humans understanding God is like fish understanding the water they're swimming in." Religious dogma on who God is and what *He wants* can be amusing and often dangerous as hell.

Therefore, the most one can hope for is to *become one with The Force.* Dropping your hands and taking a breath (entering *The Space),* then, means surrendering the Individual Mind and becoming immersed in Universal Mind. Do I want to be one lone drop of water trying to avoid drying up? Or do I want the eternal sustenance of being a drop in the ocean? When that ocean is the ocean of sound, believe me, you are in heaven! Lose the boundaries of individual perception and become quenched and drenched in the nectar of Supreme Love, Supreme Flow. Or, as a musician, luxuriate in the *Supreme Sound.*

To lose the line of definition where you end and the universe begins is an exalted state. Most of the world's most profound art emanates from there. In fact, when we endorse even the darkest actions on this planet as also being the property of Divine Consciousness, we have reached the *endgame.* We have gotten off the seesaw of good and evil and we are filled with divine perception, the non-duality spoken of previously.

———

Having said all this, let me assure you, I am not there. But I have my moments. In my music I have the perception that *every sound I hear is the most beautiful sound I've ever heard.* Again, I say, *it can be taught, it can be learned!* Every act, then, is an act of grace. Does it mean I accept all events passively? No, but it means in all my actions, I *seek* to react with grace, compassion, and enthusiasm, even though I often fall short.

The main element that stands in our way is fear—fear of getting hurt, fear of pain, fear of aggression, fear of failure, fear of dying alone, fear of not being taken care of. But when we are enveloped by Universal Mind, those fears evaporate. That I am having those moments is not in doubt. The whole ball game is extending the time that I can spend in that state. Actions encourage ownership, a desire for success and a hunger for more. How to act without disconnecting from The Source is the key.

A paradox: *The best way to do something is to surrender the need to do anything.* Those actions are moment-to-moment, never overwhelming, and are always pregnant with possibilities. A drop of action while connected to Universal Mind is worth an ocean of "strategies."

Western religion touches on being empty to receive grace. As I pointed out in chapter four, the St Francis prayer says, "Lord, make me an instrument of your peace." If the Lord of St. Francis is mercy, love, and compassion, then you *surrender* to acquire those attributes. Any plumber or internet provider can tell you that for a channel to work, it has to be unclogged. That part of the Lord's Prayer, "Give us this day our daily bread," refers to emptiness as well. If we had bread, we wouldn't be praying for it to be given. The phrase, *"Thy will, not mine, be done,"* requires detachment. Detachment from what? From my own will. Remaining empty invites fulfillment. Lack of expectations is being empty (of expectations.) Paradoxically, it frees one to take actions, and it can be practiced and acquired.

Whether one embraces biblical imagery or not, (which I neither endorse nor oppose), the idea is I remain empty of my own selfish desires or my own limiting thoughts, so that I may be filled with expanded awareness. Even a prayer for divine inspiration can clog the channel through which one can *actually receive divine inspiration.* We have to distinguish between prayer and desire, which is even trickier.

Many prayers contain the caveat: *"If it be Thy Will."* When one's life is going the way one wants, it's all, *"Thy will, not mine, be done."* But when life takes turns we don't want or appreciate, or that we even dread, we become agnostics. *"Why hast thou forsaken me? Is there really a God? If there is, does He care about me at all? Then why is He doing this?"* (Not going to attempt to answer that one!)

I am intrigued by a rather immature level of worship. Imagine if you will, a baseball player. The bases are loaded, there are two outs in the bottom of the ninth, and BOOM!— the batter hits a grand slam home run. As he crosses the plate, you see the player's unshakable love of God exhibited with *great humility* by pointing into the air as if in gratitude to the Giver of all home runs: God. I don't believe that I've ever seen a batter point to the sky in gratitude if he strikes out. Being equally grateful for failure as well as for success is much more authentic and often leads to greater success. Enlightenment is also a brilliant strategy!

Food for thought:

The musician who prepares to be the instrument has a choice. Should he block divine intervention with desire, or should he let *It* play? This changes the equation. When I practice precision or form, my goal is *not* playing well. My goal is mastery, to allow the music to play itself so I can watch from *The Space*. I can receive. There are greater sources to consult with than a piano player about such things, but I have experienced this state entirely in music.

I am also known for exhibiting these characteristics when I play. When one becomes the vehicle, it liberates the others who are listening. Staying in the moment and being guided by Universal Mind draws seekers (i.e., the audience) like "moths to the flame." I found I had an equal gift of being able to explain it and helping to bring it out in other people's voices, which is actually rarer. These concepts have greatly enhanced the power of my music. I hope writing about it will extend the power of your *life's music,* your true purpose in life.

I would like to quote a few sources from my personal course of study that is based on Kashmir Shaivism,[1] an ancient yogic philosophic tradition. A daily meditation book I read is, "Resonate with Stillness."[2] It contains quotes from two great gurus from the Siddha Yoga Path:[3] Gurumayi Chidvilasananda and Swami[4] Muktananda.[5]

In one of the daily quotes Muktananda says, "Do not think 'I am this' or 'I am that.' These kinds of feelings are

1   Kashmir Shaivism Kashmir Shaivism or more accurately Trika Shaivism refers to a nondualist tradition of Śaiva-Śakta Tantra which originated sometime after 850 CE.

2   Resonate With Stillness: Daily contemplations from quotes of Siddha Yoga Masters Gurumayi Chidvilasananda and Swami Muktananda

3   Siddha Yoga: Siddha Yoga is a path of inner transformation and discipline. It is imbued with the grace of the Siddha Yoga Guru

4   Gurumayi Chidvilasananda: The Siddha Guru and spiritual head of the Siddha Yoga Path, chosen by Swami Muktananda to become the spiritual head of Siddha Yoga after his passing.

5   Swami Muktananda: the founder of Siddha Yoga. He was a disciple and the successor of Bhagavan Nityananda.

transitory. When you are playing a certain role, you have a certain name, but it is not the ultimate truth.[6] In order to experience the ultimate truth, one must detach from transitory roles and names. In other words, one should empty oneself of their limited vision for the ultimate truth to arise within. I wouldn't say 'to enter' because it's already there."

Gurumayi Chidvilasananda said, "When do you receive everything? When you are totally empty. Simplicity is of the utmost importance."[7] One needs only to empty oneself of distractions, limited thoughts, and emotions, and then they will feel what has been there all along—the quiet, yet *tumultuous power of consciousness.*

Kashmir Shaivism teaches that the whole universe is Shiva. Shiva manifests the universe. Much of the writings feature *sutras,* or truths, that detail the nature of consciousness. A Swami on this path, and one whom I consider a friend, Swami Shantananda,[8] has written an incredible book titled, "The Splendor of Recognition," a commentary on the *Pratyabhijna-hrdayam.*[9] The *Pratyabhijna-hrdayam* is an ancient text from the 11th century, written by Kṣemarāja[10] and comprised of twenty *sutras,* or precepts, on the Ancient Science of the Soul. I found passages that are so relevant for our purposes. I'll just lift a few quotes.

He writes, "Sutra 4 tells us that everything exists within

---

6   Resonate with Stillness, December 19
7   Resonate with Stillness, November 30
8   Swami Shantananda: A Siddha Yoga monk and teacher. Wrote a book of commentaries on Pratyabhijna-hrdayam
9   Pratyabhijna-hrdayam: A key text of Kashnir Shaivism. Means "The Heart of Recognition," written by the sage Kshemaraja in the 11th century
10   Kṣemarāja: Rajanaka Kṣemarāja (क्षेमराज) (late 10th to early 11th century) was a philosopher and brilliant disciple of Abhinavagupta, who was a peerless master of tantra, yoga, poetics, and dramaturgy.

us—even one whose nature is consciousness in a contracted state"[11]—which is another way of saying in the individual state. The sutra goes on to say that in spite of this contraction, the individual "embodies the universe in a contracted form."[12] This is a marvelous statement. If all of us embody the universe, then it's not a matter of who has the magic and who doesn't. It's more about who *realizes it.* In other words, everyone that wants it can have it, if they practice perceiving it. In that case, *what human doesn't have genius inside?*

Psychedelics gave me this sensation many times and quickly, without work. The problem is that it was a window towards growth, not growth itself. Unfortunately, after the drug wears off, the spiritual attainment recedes. It becomes more of an echo. As I've said before (not above quoting myself), the great sin of drugs is that the feeling doesn't last; much like they used to joke about Chinese food—that you're hungry again two hours later. If we could all pop one pill and embody the universe forever, we'd all do it. I assure you there's nobody who doesn't want this feeling. But to embody that state, one has to become a vessel, which unfortunately takes work.

The title of chapter five is itself quotable. "Universal Consciousness Descends to Become the Mind."[13] That's beautiful! It indicates a willingness of the Universal Mind to contract into the form of the individual mind. The sutra states, "Consciousness herself, having descended from the expanded state, becomes the mind, contracted by the objects of perception."[14] The question as a musician, scientist,

11   The Splendor of Recognition p. 92
12   The Splendor of Recognition p. 92
13   The Splendor of Recognition p. 109
14   The Splendor of Recognition p. 111

laborer, monk or even politician is, how much will one focus on objects of perception and how much will one merge with the expanded state? This is the choice we have. It doesn't feel like a choice because we are often swept up by, for example, fear of consequences. That's why it's so helpful to create a safe environment to *practice letting go*—if nothing else, just to practice *recklessness* and allow it to inform our responsible actions. A musician should aim towards complete identification with the Supreme regardless of sounding bad or good.

(This is heresy!)

Becoming more aware of the expanded state can feel like swimming against the tide. It can actually feel counter-intuitive. It seems so much more familiar identifying with our contracted thoughts, like surrendering to gravity. But actions steadily taken towards a certain result will bring the changes that we desire. Or, as a friend and mentor of mine often says to me, "The only way to change a habit is to change a habit." Unfortunately, we can't just snap our fingers and change it. Well, maybe we can, but we can't just snap our fingers and *keep the change*—that's for sure. Artists of any medium can see the benefits of this idea. Even our thoughts and actions can be silver-lined by this awareness. Here is an example Swami Shantananda gives of the value. He is quoting Gurumayi Chidvilasananda here:

"In our life, everything depends on our attitude—the way we think, the way we speak, the way we hear."[15] This understanding could be the difference between life or lifelessness.

How does the individual mind graduate to Universal Mind? Swami Shantananda writes, "The universe that was previously seen as a blur comes into such sharp focus that

15   The Splendor of Recognition p. 114

our awareness of ourselves as subject pales before it. At this level, perception does not happen with the senses or the mental instruments, for these do not function in the pure creation. Perception occurs through the witnessing capacity of unencumbered consciousness."[16]

Wow! Can you believe this was written in the 11th century? I must share the Dalai Lama's concern as to whether humanity is evolving or devolving! Connecting with Universal Mind is what the individual mind longs for. It often seeks love in "all the wrong places," to quote the old song. There are various "objects of perception" that disguise true longing for the Inner Connection. But truly speaking, we are never disconnected. We seek to attain what we already have. Universal Mind means Universal Consciousness. We have always been connected, but through practice we become *conscious* of that fact. Why all the capitals, you may ask? Because in our culture when we write the name of God we capitalize! *In God We Capitalize!* These various terms are synonyms.

The human mind is a truly wondrous thing. We may never totally understand the mysteries of what's at play. Many people are absolutely convinced of the existence of God. Even the Universal Mind is still an assumption for most, but connecting with it is an empirical experience. The heightened experience is measurable, regardless of what it's attributed to. The human mind is such a powerful and expansive entity. We truly can't be sure if we are in touch with an actual deity, or if we have simply activated a different, less traveled region of our brain.

Whereas I am not sure of what kind of God actually exists, I've had ample evidence of some form of connectivity

between my individual mind and The Expanse, between nature and myself, and certainly between myself and other
musicians. I've had many, many examples of that. It can be
witnessed in how people think of the same thing at the same
time: "I was just going to call you and you called me." I've
seen amazing things on my adopted spiritual path. I've seen
results that extend far beyond normal occurrences, results
that couldn't have happened if there weren't some kind of
unseen connectivity between all things.

Again, in my studies this is called *The Shakti*. Whatever
that Force is and whatever we call it, we are always connected to it, whether conscious of it or not. Religious and
spiritual paths are filled with stories of miracles, not just
ones we read about in the Bible. I've witnessed miracles
and I've experienced miracles onstage with other musicians. I think it's one of the things that fascinates the audience. Miracles do happen onstage. We're improvising, which
means that we're playing things that actually don't exist in
any written form, and things come together typically with no
warning. We laugh and look at each other with the thought,
"How did that just happen?" Musical ESP compels us to believe that there is some form of connectivity when we open
that channel. I believe musicians who are aware of this can
help people in other walks of life open themselves up to "The
Channel."

On another date in *Resonate with Stillness*, Swami
Muktananda says it so beautifully: "In the *Bhagavad Gita*,
Lord Krishna says that the same being stretches in all direc-
tions. All activities and pursuits, all names and forms, are
only different manifestations of the Truth. Because this is
the case, there is no work that is an obstacle on the spiritual path. Anyone who worships God while following his vo-

cation is fulfilling the purpose of his birth. For example, a musician can worship God with music, provided that he has no selfish motive. A teacher can worship God by teaching, provided that he teaches selflessly. A businessman can worship God in his business, provided that he does it without selfish motive. A farmer can worship God by raising crops, provided that he does it selflessly. Doing one's work selflessly means dedicating it to God. No matter what your pursuit in the world, if you dedicate it to God, it becomes a spiritual pursuit."[17]

Whoa, that sounds pretty religious. I can hear my friends as they read this, knowing me. But let's transpose some of the language to the idea of left brain/right brain or Individual Mind/Universal Mind. Anyone who stays *connected to his right brain following his vocation* is fulfilling the purpose of his birth. A businessman can be in Universal Mind in his business, etc. No matter what your pursuit in the world, *if you do it while being conscious of Consciousness,* it becomes a spiritual pursuit.

We are happier and more content when we are in contact with Universal Mind. For musicians, scientists, golfers, bricklayers, or garbage collectors performing one's actions with consciousness of Universal Mind renders all actions sacred. We learn to watch our mind rather than be imprisoned by it. I've seen workers in restrictive jobs show their apathy and disdain in serving the public. I've seen others doing the same work with a smile or an air of friendliness or even enjoying being of service. It's not uncommon for many of those to consider themselves "born again."

A question we, as a human race, have grappled with for

17   Resonate with Stillness Swami Muktananda, December 22

all time is, if God is so great, if God is so compassionate and unerring, why do we have so much pain and suffering? When we are in perfect harmony, it's God, and when we torture and kill each other, it's supposed to be us. The irony is that in both states of mind we are looking for the same thing: *completion and connection.* (Salvation?) I really bristle at this admission, but I have arrived at that conclusion. My father used to say all the time, "If you want to give God the credit, you have to also give him the blame." I heard that so many times and, in a sense, it's pretty hard logic to refute.

That belief is so deep it feels cellular to me. But the fact is that when we're in touch with Universal Mind, love is not something to attain, but is simply present. When we are separate, we contract into *self-consciousness.* Fear and unhealthy competition ensue. *Unhealthy competition,* I like that phrase. We are usually aware of the phrase, "healthy competition." Healthy competition is, "I will do my best and you will do your best and the results will be for the best." Unhealthy competition is, "I will bury you using every bit of leverage I can find."

Our American democracy has become an unhealthy competition. "I will benefit and I will not feel safe until you are completely subjugated" is more the norm, I'm afraid. Many of us at this time in history are fearful because of this sad state of affairs. But the fact is, the only power we have to change it or our lives, is to work on strengthening our connection to Universal Mind. Whether it works or not, all of our actions will have some benefit. We can even detach from our need to exist as a species. That allows us to rise above and accomplish purposes beyond music itself. Music is more powerful when it's motivated by something larger than itself. Perhaps my connection to Universal Mind will resonate with others and that may manifest in the physical world, leading to change. *And therein lies the potential for my music to be relevant to the world.* Perhaps we won't have to dumb it down to be relevant.

A more quantifiable benefit is that I can improve the inner landscape of my own mind. Then outer conditions would not prevent me from realizing the Supreme Joy that I believe exists within me. I can experience joy and creativity for the days I may have left on this earth. I do have a choice. The choice is to struggle within the constraints of my individual mind, my thoughts—or I can continue to cultivate a connection to my right brain; to allow my individual mind to merge with the Universal Mind.

11 ■ The Steps to Effortless Mastery

Precision—Ease

Ease—Precision

Effortless—Mastery

Now that I've presented the various premises for living and acting from one state of mind or the other, I will state the original Four Steps of *Effortless Mastery*. They sit firmly on the shoulders of thousands of years of philosophy and spirituality, but are uniquely applied to the playing of a musical instrument:

Step 1: Touching the instrument from *The Space*

This is following your breath or staring at a spot on the wall, generally pulling your mind away from the act while the body (hands, feet, embouchure) touches the instrument and plays a note. You hear the note, but don't feel responsible for it. You don't need to react and you don't need to improve upon it. It is as uncluttered with human intention as when one branch of a tree touches another. The reaction one has to the sound is the same as the reaction to hearing traffic out the window. In other words, *you are not responsible for the sound and there's nothing you need to do to shape the sound in any way.* When you feel the urge to control/improve, develop, judge in any way, **put down the instrument and go back to The Space.**

Some thoughts on the 1st step

If this were a way of life one would realize mastery in the shortest possible time.

Don't confuse the first step with "relaxation exercises." Then the mind subtly devalues the first step.

Is it releasing control entirely to another "entity?" Part of the brain? A "deity" of some kind? Doesn't matter.

The first step is surrendering control, touching without thinking. It requires some degree of faith that if you let go, someone or something will catch you.

The results from the first step are fantastic. Playing becomes "irrationally" easy. One collides with one's own belief system. "Playing the _____ shouldn't be this easy.

The first step is magical. . . . Take it on faith. It's the seed that gives birth to the idea of "Becoming The Instrument."

And through all of the above, neurological pathways are altered.

Step 2: Moving around the instrument from *The Space*

Now we up the ante, turn up the heat. Now it's not just the playing of one note from *The Space,* but we allow "the body" to choose notes, move around. As your body (hands, feet, embouchure) chooses notes, one sits in a space of non-action, non-doership. The body is playing the sound emanating from the instrument and the mind is only observing, if even that. Not even paying attention to it is also an option. As soon as the mind reacts, one **drops the hands or puts down the instrument and goes back to The Space.**

Some thoughts on the second step

This process is graced by the inner space learned in the first step.

The second step is a fantasy. Wiggle your fingers in the air furiously. Imagine that you are playing the fastest and most intricate patterns with abandon. This is not a mere indulgence. The moving of fingers quickly in the air creates neurological pathways in the brain, motor skill in the body. Sometimes I imagine the raw movement is language unto itself!

The second step creates the free movement. It liberates your technique in performance.

We have restricted our fingers all our lives trying to play "correctly." We lose touch with the basic feeling of finger movement and the natural speed the fingers possess.

There is no inner groove to careful movement.

Wiggling fingers or arms (for drummers) in the air carelessly in the vague shape of playing a particular instrument "greases the joints" to play real stuff with much more efficiency.

For improvisors, the second step liberates the player to throw notes out into the void and have their resolutions appear in midair, so to speak.

I see a whole method of practice in miming—movement without the burden of being specific. Practicing flight without flight patterns.

When you get too bogged down in specifics, release yourself to the fantasy of Step Two.

Imagine if you spent a few moments everyday letting yourself play whatever notes want to come out and drinking in their sound, from the worst to the best, with total love and gratitude. Imagine if you brainwashed yourself to feel that **"Every note I play is the most beautiful sound I've ever heard."**

If this were a lifelong practice, what would your music become? How deep would your sound be, (How Deep Is the Ocean?) your connection to the instrument? Music and you would cease to be separate. You would be music. Every sound would be The Divine Music.

The second step is a model for a natural state of ecstasy for a musician. Touching the instrument becomes an open door. It manifests on contact.

And . . . **You don't even have to be a musician to experience it!**

The second step is the ritual, you are the sacrifice. You're offering right and wrong, good and bad into the fire. Liberation from judgment makes you an all-powerful extension—of The All Powerful.

Step two is the foundation.

Let it be daydreams. There is no goal to a daydream. Just "swim in the dream."

When you take a nap do you wonder what it's leading to? You simply refresh yourself and move on. Do the second step that way.

Don't let the profound results jar you. Keep doing this simple, mystical step over and over and create a brilliant life.

Step 3: Playing form, time, rhythm, harmony, or written material, etc. from *The Space*

For this step, the player chooses a specific piece of music that they know very well. It's absolutely essential that they know it like the back of their hand because to play it from *The Space* will mean to play it completely without thought or reaction, without managing the piece. It feels like *the piece is playing itself.* The goal is for that to be an actual experience, not just a nice sounding philosophy.

When one begins to play the piece, they may find that the parameters of what they can do are more modest than they assume. For example, if they play a classical piece that they feel they have mastered, once in *The Space* they may find that the piece wants to be played much slower than it's supposed to. In order to sit back and observe the piece being played, they may have to adjust the tempo to one in which they can let the body play it. If they're improvising on a jazz piece, they may find they can play a quarter of what they thought they could. Eighth notes may not be playable from

The Space, but half notes may be, or even whole notes. That's how basic their playing may become when they allow it to be played from *The Space.* At that point there's a great temptation to jump in and take control of the piece so they can feel good about their level (ego), but when the urge to control arises, ***drop the hands, put down the instrument, and go back to The Space.***

Weird, huh? As soon as you add any intentionality or care, *you detach from the instrument!* The third step is the transition from managing the music to letting the body play, freeing the mind and the spirit.

Some thoughts on the third step

Behind the performance of the third step is the shadow of the second step.

You make your offering of the third step, the performance, on the carpet of the second step, absolute love of any note you might play . . .or play by mistake.

Acceptance – of what you can and cannot play from *The Space* – leads to what needs practice in the fourth step.

The lesson to be learned in the third step is how to stay in balance and let the body play.

The third step is watching oneself play. If you accept what you can play, what comes out begins to flow.

Many musicians crumble under the weight of discontent. By indulging in dissatisfaction, one gets farther away. Therefore, loving the sound of what comes is the starting point for change.

In self-acceptance there is balance, and from that balance one gently adds new information into one's playing without disturbing the main point, which is enjoying one's self.

Step three is an honest inventory of where you're at. It sets up a clear, focused approach to practicing.

Step 4: Practicing from *The Space*

By step four one is ready to do technical work from the same space. There's a way to do this that is well outlined in my first book. In fact, I recommend reading the chapters on all the steps. I demonstrate these steps in many videos that can be found on my YouTube channel and elsewhere.[1] The point is that without mental interference, which one has been practicing in the first three steps, highly technical movement can become muscle memory. One could argue that precision *is not acquired* until it has been become muscle memory. The gift of music doesn't really begin until material is played easily. If one has to "manage" the material too carefully, it blocks all further promise. The fourth step trains the body.

Some thoughts on the fourth step

When we listen objectively to our playing, sparing ourselves the drama of emotional response (third step), we can focus on the removal of obstacles to our expression and attain new levels of technical freedom. That is step four.

The fourth step is not a linear approach to practice. We are not "rehearsing" material to be inserted into the music. We are forming

---

1 A particularly great video for a discussion and demonstration of the four steps is a video I did for jazzheaven.com titled, "*Effortless Mastery*, The 4 Steps."

inroads of familiarity with musical patterns or patterns of thought, with motor functions and muscle memory.

Each exercise is an opportunity to create effortless precision. Work on small examples and when one is "absorbed," come up with variations so one can begin again.

When playing classical music, focus the fourth step on the most difficult passages and notice not only greater ease in those spots, but greater ease in the entire piece!

You are training the body, establishing new capabilities.

The first and second steps provide the mental backdrop for the fourth step. Those two steps remind you what effortless and thought-free playing feels like.

Don't look for the studies to end. Imagine you were endlessly upgrading, creating mastery again and again.

Each "snarl" in your technique like a knot in a muscle. The masseuse works on that spot until the knot is undone and the blood is flowing. Trust that any passage, no matter its difficulty, can be played with ease. Let the body figure it out.

Don't look for improvement in your playing. Just do the exercise and retreat. In fact, the dance step is, work the passage and retreat . . . work and retreat . . . work and retreat. The retreat gives the work a chance to seep into the subconscious and program the muscles.

The fruits of the practice will be felt as an effect on, rather than a rehearsal of, the performance. You'll feel your playing evolving.

Misunderstandings about the steps to Effortless Mastery

That it has to be spiritual. It's spiritual if you want it to be. It can just be a very practical way to get past your blocks—psychologically, physically, emotionally and technically.

That you have to practice the steps perfectly or they don't work. As they say AA, "It's progress, not perfection." Even the attempt to meditate is meditation. Allowing yourself to touch the instrument from a general state of release is still moving towards the goal.

That you have to play "from The Space" at concerts and everywhere you play. No! This is the most common misconception. When playing, if you want to get mad, get mad. If you want to try, try; if you want to care, care. But keep doing the exercises and changes will *happen to you*.

That you'll have to do these steps for years before changing. You could do the first step today and feel liberated by nightfall.

––––––––––

We'll often get off track because the things we've been working on did not manifest in a performance situation. Most will conclude that it's not working. It may be that *it hasn't worked yet!* In that case, practicing more of the same is required. "Don't quit one day before the miracle happens," as they say.

Since I have been the Artistic Director of the Effortless Mastery Institute at the Berklee College of Music I have taught these steps as courses. We're finding that the steps help with pressing problems in the students minds and emotions. Berklee cares very deeply about this dysfunction-that-shall-never-be-named, much like Voldemort of Harry Potter fame. They have invested their trust in EMI to try and stem the tide as much as possible. In many university classes, overkill seems to be associated with value added, but it's not. An EMI teacher would coach a student towards actual ownership of the music and a more loving attitude towards themselves. We want students appreciating who they are, not constantly judging who they are. EMI is Tai Chi, Qi Gong, Body Mapping, Yoga for Musicians, and Alexander Technique. Through different methods, the goal is the same: confidence, self-love, concentration while practicing, muscle efficiency, freedom in performance. Many somatic disciplines have different goals or different ways to achieve the same goal. But they all offer a balancing of the mind. *Effortless Mastery* is then, the delivery system for the benefits of those disciplines. When one approaches their instrument, one shouldn't change their focus to their mental patterns involved with music. If one is a yoga master, then when touching the instrument, *do yoga!*

Effortless Mastery is a powerful way for the young and old to heal their wounds, rediscover their voice, dissolve mental stress, and not be overwhelmed, all while developing their art faster than before. Since it is such a direct way of expelling doubts fears and low self-value, it may prove itself to be a powerful therapy for non-musicians.

The Four Steps are blossoming into a discipline like Alexander Technique or Reiki.

Final thoughts

When a musician is trying to play a specific piece of music, the EM teacher will ask them to play it without any effort or desire to play correctly." This will freak out the musician, as if there were some risk to that, some consequence. It feels consequential to play an instrument. But if they can play the example without any effort, it is said to be mastered. " What would be the benefit to performing, in one's own mind, as if there were no consequences, without any effort to control the action? **I'm inviting a sports team to invite me to try it with them. (Yankees especially!)**

Playing without effort, without consequences allows the body to play. It's the best way to find your weakness. Playing without trying to play! This makes *Effortless Mastery* unique because most systems do not welcome failure. But what's on the other side of that? What might be revealed? Even if one doesn't't have the courage to live life that way, the concept can be practiced for 5 or 10 minutes a day, or an hour, and then return to "reality." That will integrate the newly found freedom into a life of structure. Freedom within form is the absolute highest attainment in any field.

It can be practiced in the extreme when there are no consequences. At a safe time from a safe place, *complete irresponsibility*. Like a therapy. Then one can just observe how, and if, it filters into their structured environment. It takes a lot of energy to constantly judge oneself.

Sometimes *Effortless Mastery* is a physical therapy. sometimes akin to psychotherapy, or it may become a spiritual path. EMI could be a place where philosophical, spiritual and holistic ideas are bantered about, a place where musicians ponder those ideas *with the instrument in their hands*. A spa, an ashram, a place of serious self-discovery and a place to work on skills from an expanded consciousness. Symposiums and retreats providing a place where we remain conscious of the source of music, sound, vibration, the source of our lives. It can indeed be ***an enlightened center for musicianship.*** Perhaps *Effortless Mastery* can make a meaningful contribution to the world.

12 ■ Muscle Memory
Training the muscles or the mind through repetition

You're in *The Space,* loving your mistakes and transformed. You're in your right brain. You're God's right-hand man! He will grant a miracle and *you'll be a virtuoso without any effort.* Isn't this what *Effortless Mastery* means? *Hell, no!* Here's what I didn't say in my first book: ***It takes a lot of effort to become effortless!***

I wish I had because many misinterpreted that book to mean that one did not have to practice to acquire virtuosity. They felt it completely sidestepped the issue of practice and study. As I said in the introduction, when they read the book, they were typically entertained by the first part. In that section I addressed the way we think and all the ways we self-sabotage. I described, humorously sometimes, exactly how we procrastinate and how fear leads to avoidance. I outlined how ego ruins our practicing and playing. But very often people didn't take the second part seriously: *the solution.* That was the Four Steps. The fourth step is the most conscious practice towards precision one could ever conceive of. In fact, it takes the first three steps to prepare the mind to be able to practice on this level. Let me state it again briefly:

Step 4: Practicing from *The Space*

Now this one step is the key! Let's take a look at Step Four because it is the answer to the very reasonable question, how will I acquire skill if I don't work at it? Ah, but you *do* work at it! You just work at it with more perfect focus and in greater detail than ever before. In fact, you become so much more thorough in knowing what to work on and how deeply one must work. You also find out truly, how long something needs to be worked on—*until one has mastered it!* The fourth step creates muscle memory.

Here I will quote my first book:

> **Step 4: Chapter 20.** ". . . the question naturally comes up: 'If I'm to accept whatever wants to come out, then how do I improve on what I am playing? . . .'
>
> As stated earlier, mastery is not about being able to play something correctly most of the time, or even all of the time. Mastery is being able to play it perfectly every time *without thought.* Now that you're able to retain the awareness of "the inner space" while performing actions, achieving mastery over new technical things really becomes possible."[1] Technical mastery depends on muscle memory and motor skills. I quoted *Zen and The Art of Archery* several times in the first book. One of those quotes was: "This state of unconsciousness is realized only when,

---

1 *Effortless Mastery* p. 157

completely empty and rid of the self, he becomes one with the *perfecting of his technical skill.*"[2]

Let's take that statement apart for a moment. This "state of unconsciousness" is *The Space.* Some would argue that it is consciousness, not unconsciousness, but that is semantics. The point is, the state that one aspires to is only realized when one is "completely empty and rid of the self." The self (small "s") being expressed here is the conscious mind, that part of us that controls us with *desires.* The other incredible realization in this statement is the fact that one must empty oneself of ego *before* "he becomes one with the perfecting of his technical skill." A non-spiritual synonym for that is muscle memory. The action is locked in and therefore easy. As stated earlier, you've used a fork thousands of times. Ever miss your mouth? Allowing for those that might have been too drunk to find it, let's say you've only missed it five out of 70,000 times. I call that muscle memory! Mastery!

So often, we associate mastery as the final phase of accomplishment—but mastery should be the starting point. One should establish a physical relationship to the instrument based on muscle memory. The earlier we learn muscle memory of the basic elements of a given skill, the more successful we're likely to be as we progress. Mastery of *one's own mind* makes the goal more attainable. We're really going to need a steadfastness because we weren't taught that way as children. In other words, we fall short in our preparation *because of the restlessness of our minds!* Impatience, doubting our ability, self-criticism, and the up and down self-valuing

2   *Effortless Mastery* quoting Eugene Herrigel, *Zen in The Art of Archery* p. 38

of ourselves causes us to study or practice in a way that almost ensures the non-completion of tasks.

Sometimes lack of muscle memory leads to inhibition. One is being careful because they can't play the music securely. If they "let go" they may get lost. I've heard lectures by great musicians encouraging the most philosophical or even spiritual concepts related to playing. Hungry for that freedom, sincere music students are hanging on every word and often thinking to themselves, "Why don't I have those experiences?" or "Why can't I go there?" Very often the problem is not your imagination, *it's the fact that it still takes too much effort to function!* Physical requirements have not yet become muscle memory. Too much effort to keep the form, too much effort to play on chords. in tempo or with rhythm, etc. Too much effort to play the classical piece. The effort it takes for you to hold it together is the block *between you and the greater possibilities.*

Lack of muscle memory usually solves the mystery of why you don't play better. Two people might be able to play on the same level. Why does one sound better? Because what one does without too much effort the other really has to concentrate to play. The philosophy of music is premature before the technical elements are automated. This is one of the huge gaps in jazz education I've witnessed time and time again. One can downgrade the sophistication of the material they play to a simpler music and feel free. No one *has to get more complex. Who cares?* But if one aspires to the more sophisticated technology of say, jazz, they will not experience creativity while stumbling over fundamentals. Therefore, the encouragement the great musicians should be giving the students is to really nail the fundamentals. Not attaining muscle memory on the basics will be the reason they won't attain their dreams. Getting older doesn't fix it. When the fundamentals are muscle memory, the player is free!

I'd like to tell a few stories that illustrate this:

When I was in college at Berklee, I would often go to one of the great jazz clubs at that time, the Jazz Workshop. It was there that I first heard live the likes of Bill Evans, Chick Corea, and McCoy Tyner. I remember going to see McCoy Tyner every night. At that time, he was the most "burning" piano player alive. (That means the strongest finger technique and the strongest rhythm!) His single notes were like hammers, like a vibraphonist would smack the metal bars with individual mallets. On this level McCoy burned with his fingers. Now if I went every night, it seemed that McCoy was that burning every time. There was never a time where his rhythm was weaker and his fingers less like hammers. I had to contemplate this. Why would he perform on this level always, without fail? Why would I think that even if he thought he had a bad night? There was only one logical answer. *It must be easy!* Nothing else could really explain it. That is muscle memory. That's why McCoy Tyner sounded that burning every night.

The same thing happened with Bill Evans. I went to see him every night and he had honed his harmonic movement into pure muscle memory. Every night Bill Evans played perfect harmony and what we call voicings, the notes that express the harmony. How did he do that? The answer is, his muscles, in perfect communication with his mind, performed those harmonies as if they were single notes. I did not get a chance to see Herbie Hancock. He was too famous to play the Jazz Workshop, but whenever I did see him in concert, I noticed that his rhythm, far more developed than mine, was played with the same ease that one would play a whole note with no rhythm.

There are people who are creative when the music is rubato.[3] As long as there's no time or rhythm, they can be very creative. That's why, humorously, inferior players are suddenly very free on the last note of a song. That's because there's a big fermata[4] on top of that last note. If the music were in time, in form or very rhythmic, that person would be all twisted up inside. After contemplating this again, I arrived at the conclusion that Herbie Hancock played rhythm with the comfort in his body that I played a whole note. Refinement of rhythm comes down to the smallest unit, and the muscles become effortlessly comfortable with that unit.

Maybe only musicians will understand this next bit. But the proof that muscle memory is the key factor is this. Ask McCoy to play what he played in an unfamiliar odd meter, or with a pattern other than the ones his right hand had absorbed. *He wouldn't sound like McCoy!* Ask Bill Evans to play everything in another key a half-step higher. Suddenly those harmonies and voicings wouldn't be so locked in. Muscle memory is the great fact that's not really talked about. Ask any jazz musician to play blues in B instead of Bb! jazz players get my meaning here.

Another story: Once I was playing the wedding of a good friend of mine, Gene Perla, the great bass player who had played with Elvin Jones for many years. He and Jan Hammer[5] co-owned a farm in upstate New York. Gene asked me to put a band together to play for his wedding. I put a really nice band together and I played a Fender Rhodes electric piano out in the backyard. I was playing great that day

3   Rubato: out of tempo
4   Fermata: a hold on a particular note
5   Great pianist and keyboardist. Scored the music to *Miami Vice* TV show and was keyboardist in the Mahavishnu Orchestra

and everyone came up to me to tell me that. Jan Hammer, himself one of the greatest pianists, told me I sounded great. I felt wonderful. At the end of the day some percussionists came marching down the street to join the party. They were playing some heavy stuff. I don't know how I would've fared with them. Jan Hammer, like Chick Corea or McCoy Tyner, is one of the most rhythmic pianists.

When the percussionists arrived, Jan opened his basement and rolled out his B3 organ.[6] Jan had been partying and had not touched the instrument all day. Yet, when the B3 was plugged in and ready to go, he started playing with those percussionists at a level above where my playing was at the end of the day. In other words, the muscle memory that Jan and Herbie had for rhythm started above where mine left off. After contemplating this, I realized that I should go back to the beginning with my rhythm—back to the fundamentals—and teach my muscles to play, or allow them to learn to play on a higher level. This I have done for decades. I don't know if I have attained Jan's level, but I know I've improved mine 1,000 percent. What the stories illustrate is that the level of one player versus another may just come down to the level of muscle memory, or *level of ease* one or the other has achieved.

One can easily see the parallels in any other skill. It may not be mastery of music, but perhaps a mastery of facts pertaining to a given subject. It could be mastery of details, or it could be mastery of muscular movement, as in sports. The golf club must swing itself. I'd love to work *Effortless Mastery* with a golfer and try having him *not be attached to hitting the ball* and wait for the body to hit it! (Yankees, take note!)

6   The legendary gospel and jazz organ made by Hammond

The body is the instrument that swings the golf club. Patient repetition leads to muscle memory. It has to. The only repetition that doesn't lead to that result is *impatient repetition*. Repetition of key aspects, such as a pitcher in baseball repeating his arm angle, or as they say, arm slot, depends solely on if it has become muscle memory.

That may be the point where Zen philosophy becomes relevant. Gaining consistency and not succumbing to pressure may rely on practicing the muscle movements again and again. The reason one can hang in there is that they are not pressuring themselves for results, just showing up for the work. That is what the Zen statement refers to as *"empty and rid of the self."* For the ball to find the hole, one must become a master of the technique involved, but one must master himself to continue to apply the training *without expectations*. I dare say sports is eons ahead of music in this regard.

I refer to the first book again:

"Step Four requires you to take small samples of things you can't quite execute, and absorb them on a level of mastery. It combines the effortlessness of Step One and the freedom of movement of Step Two, and applies these to specific examples of things you can't do ⊠ familiarizing yourself with something rhythmic, harmonic, or melodic on such a deep level that it feels as though you are just wiggling your fingers." (Guess what? *It takes an extremely balanced mind to practice that way!*)

"This practicing must be very focused, very intentional. The length of time you practice is limited to the length of time you can remain in *The Space*. Then you must STOP or you will compromise the deliberateness of the practice. In this way, five or ten minutes of practice is preferable to two hours of rambling."[7] This can be a template for any kind of attainment of skills, mental or physical. *Effortless Mastery* could be a powerful therapy for any endeavor.

The power of practice

It may seem like pie in the sky, but it's actually more of a trick question. Would you rather accomplish a lot in your practice or practice from a mind? The trick is, from a centered mind one will accomplish more and what one learns will be much more secure. It doesn't necessarily happen on one's timeline, which is based on ego more than reality. Would you rather play great or play from a centered mind? A trick question again, because you will play better than ever when you are centered. (You'll just have to try it to see!)

When the fruits of practice do not materialize or conform to one's timeline, one becomes impatient. The practice lacks detail. The results are mediocre. The lessons have been learned to a point, but there is no muscle memory. A perfected state of mind creates a perfected study. Five or ten minutes of practice in a focused state of mind is preferable to two hours of a wandering mind. If we practice new things with enough consistency, over time we can create new patterns and forge new pathways of action in the brain. If we hang in there, we may even develop new reactions to stimuli. There really isn't another way to reroute the mind, except for possible scientific discoveries that may come. Our current understanding is that the path most well-worn is the path of

7   *Effortless Mastery* p. 160

least resistance. It explains why we do so many things that we consciously choose not to do, and vice versa.

To create a new pattern or change an old habit, the place where we often fail is in the repetition. Only enough repetition leads to the new pattern. The conscious mind tells us, "Oh, this subject is too immense, I'll never learn it." Or, having practiced something for some time, the thought might be, "I should have learned this by now." Practicing from our ego, three weeks feels like three months, three months seems a year. Those thoughts are quite self-defeating, of course. In the first instance, one won't even begin the practice because of a negative belief about its difficulty, and in the second, they won't patiently commit the time it takes to own the new information.

This also illustrates "the value of mistakes," which will be discussed in a later chapter. To establish a new intuitive pattern in the brain one may have to tread that new path repeatedly for as long as it takes for the change to occur. And that's where we often fall short. Our ego is telling us we must move on, that we need to practice something else, or it is telling us that some strategy of practice has been working for a while but has stopped working. That's the tricky part. It is like being in a new relationship. In a new relationship every sensation is one of love. After a certain amount of time, the luster wears off and the couple may go into an emotionally numb period. If they hang in there and keep practicing caring towards one another, a deeper pattern may emerge.

Now, I am no marriage counselor, so I will leave it at that. However, in music people practice something for what they consider quite a while. Then they often discover that the fruits of the practice still elude them. Discouraged, they often move on to something else, thinking that is what will save them. In fact, it is the "dead time," where it feels like nothing is happening, that one must *persevere and keep practicing*. The easiest way to do that is to remain empty, as we have been discussing. That's the irony. Empty of expectations, one just does the work of perfecting his technical skill, and doesn't wonder where he is in the process.

Anyone can learn to play music if they'll hang in there long enough. University education, I'm afraid, is one of the main culprits of dysfunctional learning. It would be truly frightening to find how many students were connected to their music *until they went to college!* Accredited schools have to place more importance on quantity than quality, on covering a certain amount of material by the end of a semester, instead of living with the material *until the result is realized.* There are skills involved in playing that will simply not respond to imaginary units of time like a week, or a semester, or four years for that matter. (This is where we might all take a peek in the mirror about whether some of these students belong in music college.) Where did we get the idea that something introduced in a week could be learned by the next? Teaching should not be exclusively the introduction of new material. Introducing new information should only be done occasionally. The rest of time, a teacher should be *coaching the aspirant towards ownership of skills.* Whether improvising on chord progressions, playing Bach, or swinging a golf club, the action must be absorbed to the point of muscle memory, and for that to happen, repetition of the action must take place, not for a week, or a semester, *but until the fruits have been realized.* Then one can perform with complete precision while attuned to *The Space. Ta da! Muscle memory!*

Changing ourselves or our habits can work similarly. Here

I must quote a sentence from Swami Shantananda's book: "It's like an idea which was seen at first as indefinite and hazy, then becomes larger than life on our mental screen as we invest it with more and more of our awareness."[8] That is the power of *extended* practice. Practice that one does for an indeterminate length of time. The length of time is irrelevant. Or perhaps it's something one studies for their whole lifetime. Maybe getting sober is painful but the literature promises joy. One quits, believing that sobriety wasn't all it was cracked up to be. But perhaps joy was *one-day away*. Hence, "Don't quit before the miracle happens."

Let me give a non-musical example of a friend of mine. He began a practice several years ago of waking up at 5 a.m. and meditating for one hour. This is something I have never been able to do. He does this every day no matter how he feels. He didn't quite see the benefits in his actions or emotional stability for years but he kept going nonetheless. In 2016, the world had a great shock. Donald Trump was elected president of the United States. Now I hope you're reading this thirty years later because perhaps you can say, "Oh, remember that history? That's when they thought this was a catastrophe. Little did they realize that he would become the greatest president of all time!" (LOL) But it is also possible you'll never this read because by your time all books will have been incinerated!

In any case, many of us went through extreme and often debilitating anxiety. My friend recognized as well as anyone the potential doom of this, but he noticed one day that he hadn't had the anxiety others were experiencing. He said to me, "For some reason, I haven't had the emotional effects of

8   The Splendor of Recognition p. 96

this election. I suddenly realized it must be the benefit of the five years I have been doing that meditation at 5 a.m." That's muscle memory on the mental landscape! He certainly didn't have the reaction I had of crawling into a fetal position for two weeks. So, the benefits of a practice he had been doing regularly for a long time, without knowing what those benefits might be, served him in the right way at the right time.

This is the power of practice that is done regularly for years without thinking about its effect. It's a great lesson for musicians who have certain gaps in their playing that would require that kind of regular effort. But it's analogous for people in all walks of life. This is best done without expectation and with consistency for as long as it takes. Just *doing without measuring*, like brushing your teeth.

Sitting at the piano, going into *The Space,* allowing my hands to rise and drift towards the keys while imagining someone or something else was moving them is a practice I've done or taught for 45 years. Teaching this technique was another blessing to me, another way to drive it deeper into my subconscious. In other words, approaching the piano and going into *The Space* is *an extremely well-worn path for me.* It's muscle memory. When I applied the first step to my life, it worked. I was shocked at how well it worked.

Whether practicing precision, absorbing knowledge, or acquiring life-coping mechanisms, patient, precise practice is vital to creating muscle memory.

13 ■ The Goals of Practice

FOG (Imagine the sound of a fog horn whenever you see the word "fog.")

As ego can cause atrophy in performance or improvisation, it can also render practicing ineffective. I can ask at a master class how many people practice and get many raised hands. Then I ask a question that they haven't thought about. "How many of you are actually improving as a result of your practicing?" There are some hands raised but they are clearly less sure. *(Fog)* If practice is approached the right way you know you're getting better because it's *getting easier.* If I ask one person if they're getting better, they might say, "I *think* so." That is ego-speak for "no," as if to say, "I'd like to think I'm getting better." *(Fog)*

Being generally overwhelmed by workload, many try to focus on a specific idea to work on while simultaneously being aware of eight other things they have to do. Sound familiar? *(Fog)* They don't know where to start, how long to work on one thing, which thing will bring them victory the fastest. *(Fog)* Older musicians may relate to this kind of . . . *Fog!*

Here is the perfect approach, but I understand that you will do them imperfectly. That's what we all do with the teacher's teachings. We do it imperfectly. Nonetheless, I must give it as the perfect idea so it can draw you *towards* perfection. If your practice embodies patience and humility then you can focus on a passage without having to move on. **Don't think of progress as moving on. Think of it as going deeper down.**

People always want to move on. That's why so many don't play an instrument securely. Not mastering things, or having intelligent use of the material, causes a downward spiral of negative beliefs. Instead of understanding that while studying in university, for example, the material is being laid out in a way that's *designed to fail*, they think *"I guess I'm not as talented as I thought I was."*

Clarity comes with ease and familiarity. Repetition from an observational state of mind fosters patience. It also allows mistakes to happen. If there is a mistake, *let it happen*. Then go in deeper to that spot and do surgery on the mistake. If you can adopt that process and it grows, you can accomplish anything. You can accomplish anything in any profession with that kind of humility. Don't push, just be present and not particularly in a hurry. Ego causes one to lose focus. Practicing with ego accomplishes the opposite of the ego's desires.

The goal of standard practice is to play the right notes correctly instead of the true goal, *to play them easily*. Each passage learned to the point of ease is a battle won. Winning the war means *becoming totally comfortable with the instrument*. The overall goal is *contact with the instrument makes you comfortable.* This is why so few learn to touch the instrument from their true self. The idea should go beyond just playing correct notes. That is like traveling half way across the river. The other half? *The piece should play itself.* Or at least it should be easy to play. How can one taste the nectar if all their attention is on trying to play the piece correctly? Playing with ease should not be an option but a fundamental goal. Then one can focus on more fun details such as emotions, impulses or even bravado. Achieving this means being willing to start over and be patient.

LESS IS MORE (Sing "Less is more" angelically on middle C.)

Becoming really familiar with one piece should trump trudging through a number of pieces. Common misguided notions that weaken our practice are often systemic in the world of education. The most fundamental is prioritizing quantity over quality. One can learn more about playing their instrument from mastering one piece than by covering several. **Less is more.**

This leads to a stunning controversy in education, music or otherwise. Is it better to cover large swaths of material in preparation for a limited checkpoint, (a *jury*, perhaps?) or is it better to narrow the information down so that true ownership of said material can be achieved? The emotional and mental benefits of the latter are enormous. Ownership of the material gives the student the feeling of confidence that they can master something. *They can play!* It builds confidence that he or she can learn. Believe me, there are more students that lose that confidence from the sheer volume of material they are required to cover. And "cover" is all they are able to do. ***Less is more.*** Quantity over quality may be more than a waste of time, it may be detrimental to one's desire to improve and express themself. I do think this may be changing as we are all groping for ways of making sure that each and every student has a meaningful experience that enhances their music and their life. That is a point worth illuminating. *Enhancing their music and their life.*

DETACHMENT (Spoken on an F#.)

Quoting my writing on the fourth step: "This is important: *the player must be willing to put the instrument down often!* This could mean releasing the instrument after each repetition, if necessary. The drummer puts his sticks down, the horn player puts the horn on the floor or on a chair, and the pianist takes his hands off the keyboard. Here again, the practice of releasing the instrument and starting again says that the player is not attached to the goal, though he patiently strives for it day after day. **He will find that if he plays once or twice and releases the instrument, takes a deep breath and starts again, the very next time will be easier and more familiar as the information 'seeps in.'** Though he is drawn towards effort, by stopping, he retreats into stillness and guides his technique into effortlessness. His ego will seduce him into trying harder, but *he should actually try less the next time.* Perfection is something you surrender to. It overcomes you. When ready to resume practicing, one should go in the opposite direction mentally. Instead of wanting to do better, the musician might even think, *"I hope I play* *it wrong!"* As weird as it sounds, such a thought may trick the mind into letting go, resulting in a surprising ease of execution."[1] *(Detachment)*

STAY FOCUSED (Repeated hypnotically over the lowest B on the piano.)

Taking many little breaks is how one can maintain focus, or *mindfulness,* as they say. (2021 update: Everything is mindfulness these days! Wellness was the previous word. It lost all meaning when it appeared on my health insurance plan. When we are offered a 10 percent discount for mindfulness that word will also become meaningless.) The best way to extend focus is to stop when you've lost it. A mini break lets you start again. Sometimes the best focus we have is at the beginning. Let many moments of practice be the beginning. Start fresh many times.

The power of attraction rather than promotion

I would like to make a pilot program for children that introduces them to instruments in a free-form way. They can explore the instruments however they want, and ask any questions they may have about how to make a sound on a particular instrument. Conventionally, the first lesson is reading notes, arguably the least fun thing about music. Most of your early teachers, and many teachers in general,

1 *Effortless Mastery* p. 160

are misguided because their focus is on moving forward. It starts as a child. As stated before, the child who becomes comfortable with one piece may play better than the one that has already finished the second book of music.

Through one piece the kid can actually discover how *to play the instrument. Reading being the first activity,* the child has no sense of the piece they are playing, they're just mechanically playing some version of the right note values. They have not had a chance to explore the instrument, their interest in it or their relationship to it. They haven't been allowed to develop any natural curiosity about the instrument. It's no wonder so many quit as soon as they have enough power to dissuade their parents.

I will now tell a story that angers my wife a bit because she remembers it differently. (How rare!) However, I'm writing the book! She was a den mother, and she and her fellow den mothers took turns hosting events for the girls in their houses. When my wife took her turn, she asked me to attend and make the theme about music. I was happy to do that. I took all my instruments and put them into the center of the room. Piano and synthesizer were against the wall. I had percussion instruments, flutes, an old trombone from high school, everything I could find.

The girls arrived one by one with their mothers and, as they came in, they saw all these instruments in the center of the room and went right to them. They shook the maracas, banged the drums, banged the piano, and one girl picked the trombone and tried every which way to make a sound. I showed her how to do that and she sounded like a fart machine almost instantly.

The children were making quite a ruckus. Some of the mothers got a little nervous. They asked if we shouldn't start the class. I said the class had already started! The enthu-siasm they were showing for the noise they were making was the essence of what it's all about! Hopefully, they would re-member this feeling when the inevitable time of lessons and structure began. I joined in playing wildly with them and it felt like playing free with my friends, except these kids were better at it, less inhibited. After a while, it quieted down and I began to explain the different instruments and they were totally into it. By the end of the session, the little girl who played the trombone had lips as big as a clown's. But she was so happy. I was delighted to find out later that in public school she had taken up the trombone!

Music is easy!

Here is another personal story. This story will reveal the whole secret of playing music. My daughter started with the piano. Then she played violin and finally found the guitar. That was the instrument she really loved to play. She was studying piano with a very good local teacher but at some point, I made the fateful decision to teach her myself. In some ways this was a big mistake because daughters have daddies wrapped around their little fingers. But I was going to teach her what I had written about in *Effortless Mastery* and focus on quality, not quantity.

If a child learns one piece securely, the benefit isn't just that one piece. The child *becomes a better player after learning that one piece.* As I described earlier, the benefit of practicing this way isn't just the spots you're working on. In fact, you're building a better infrastructure as a player that can be applied to the next piece. Anyway, back to the story.

Before I took over, I found that she wasn't playing any piece right. I mean, it was sort of right, but maybe the rhythm wasn't there, or her shoulders were hunched up to her ears with tension. Why does a seven-year-old need to learn to hunch her shoulders like an accountant of sixty-eight? A child can learn tension and anxiety later in life by being a banker or politician. They don't need to learn it through playing piano! That's why for so many children piano lessons are a negative experience.

In a sense, we're all victims of this system. Teachers, too. I like to say that teachers are students who have been wounded longer. The child barely realizes what he's playing. The teachers often feel the pressure to go on this way. First of all, they were taught this way, and secondly, they probably feel the pressure from the parents who want to see what they think is progress. The parent's idea of progress is very different from actual progress. If their child has been playing the same piece for six months, that wouldn't feel like progress, but it might be.

Now, as I said, teaching my kid myself was really not so easy! A lot of times she got out of lessons or she wasn't practicing. She had this reason, or that reason, but just like when I work with other students, we stayed with the same piece because I didn't see ownership yet. It wasn't *easy yet*. She was playing a little Vivaldi piece. I would say to her, "just go back to that spot or another spot." I think we were on that piece for about ten months, which is a long time for one piece. She would play other things that she figured out herself, but that's what we worked on. Then one day, just before we sat down to dinner, she said, "Hey dad, is this what you mean?" She played the piece looking at me, not even at the keyboard. *Her hands* played the piece. The piece swung (even classical pieces swing if you play them easily) and she kind of looked like me playing! She had it under control. Without making a fuss I said, "Yeah, that's it. You got it. Let's go eat."

You might not think of that as progress, but after that, *every piece she played on every instrument she played like that!* That's the way she played the piano, that's the way she played the violin and that's the way she played the guitar. That's the way she *expected to play.* She could have problems with certain passages on the violin, and we'd work on them together but this was now *her* approach. She knew she had to work on the passage until it *played easily.* That's the missing link! She learned that that is the only way to play an instrument. If something was difficult, she'd run it by me. She knew she must not be finished practicing it if *the music still seemed difficult!* After all, *wasn't music easy!* She got it and I thanked God she did. This is the greatly overlooked point of practice. Not just to play it correctly, but to experience the ease.

MSD

What is the deadly disease called "MSD?" It's an acronym for *Music School Disease!* What is Music School Disease? Well, it starts with being overwhelmed by too much material in each class, each teacher giving assignments without a sense of what else is being assigned in other classes, causing a buildup of material that can be overwhelming. At best, it can be *covered* but certainly not *owned.* That works in most other fields like law, medicine, etc. You see, in those fields if you haven't mastered something you can look it up, refresh your memory or what-have-you. In music, if you haven't mastered something *we can hear it!* Once you count off the tempo, the only music that comes out is music you know like the back of your hand. In real time there's no time to "look it up."

So, the first *wound* is studying things and understanding them in your head but not hearing them in your playing, which leads to disappointment and negative belief. In fact, the desire to hear those things ruins the flow of things you do know, leaving the player worse than before. Add to that the opinions, biases, constant critiquing of the students by musicians they respect, and they develop the critic inside their own head. At this point one may have contracted MSD. It goes like this. The student is so overwhelmed, confused, and over-criticized that if they play something and it comes out nice, easily, and fluid, *it must be the wrong shit!* That's right! They've lost respect for the things they *can* play.

You've heard of PTSD? Music students may get PTCD. *Post Traumatic Critique Disorder!* They are rated, critiqued, and berated with opinions from their teachers so often that they can't embrace the possibility *that their playing is fine!* What they loved has been supplanted by *what they consider valid.* There is nothing more satisfying than seeing the veil lift from those students (and quite a few teachers) as they reconnect, or in many cases *connect* for the first time, to their true voice.

I don't practice things I'm going to play. I practice things for the effect they have on my playing.

How can one be satisfied practicing a small quantity of material when the mind is constantly saying, "I have so much to practice!"? To address this reality, I like to offer the above sentence for your contemplation. Understanding it may be a valuable way of looking at anything that involves motor skills or muscle memory.

Let me explain. If one's job involves thinking on one's feet, or, as we say in the trade, *improvising,* then your ability to stream intelligent left-brained information is dependent on the courage to flow, to trust. But it is also dependent on how solid your technique is! My best example is what I know best, music. What is music? When you take away all the window dressing, styles, ethnology and sociology, it is simply, rhythm, harmony and melody. This is what all music is. Your ability to play written music, sightread, or improvise is dependent upon your familiarity, your *ease* with those elements.

If you work on one aspect, say rhythm, you might devise an exercise that has a rhythmic challenge, or goal. Learning the rhythm of this exercise would be nice, but if you master it, you might feel a difference in your rhythm when applied to other examples. You didn't work on the other things but those other things benefit from your work on this example. If you devise another exercise, different notes, same goal, rhythmic mastery of that one example, it's possible your overall rhythm improves again. Instead of thinking you have to practice each and every rhythm you might play, you stay with one thing and it raises your game so that other things require less effort.

The point of the exercises could be technique or fingering, etc. Let's say you're trying to improve your sight reading. You may practice on as little as four to eight bars. Stop, go into *The Space* and do it again, rather than trudging through long passages that fatigue you and erode your concentration. Small passages that you just go for will improve your overall ability to sightread. In classical training, it might mean staying with a rhythmic passage way past the point of playing it correctly, and imbibing it to the point of muscle memory. That muscle memory will make the next rhythmic challenge easier. Sports training usually has the right idea. The repetition of one aspect of the game benefits one's entire game. And that repetition will be much more thorough *if practiced from The Space!*

This resolves the overwhelming malaise many students feel when they can't figure out what to practice first, how many other things they need to practice, and how long it should take. If they concentrate on the same subject, one example at a time, their ability to execute naturally increases and raises their overall level of play. The goal of practicing is mastery, ownership, or at least ease.

Here's another profound benefit, very unexplored. You may work on something that you're never going to master, but patient work on it from the ground up improves many other aspects of your game! This too requires surrender. Think about it. If the conscious mind tells you, "I'm never going to get this" and it is *correct,* what's the use then? Ah, but there might be elements in the practice that improve coordination, mental agility, or in the case of music, the fundamentals of rhythm, harmony and melody. I have several of those things that I work on that may never manifest unto themselves, but I have seen so much improvement in related areas.

This can be applied to any area of study, but the example I'm about to give is for musicians. (Again, I'm writing this book *because* of what I've learned from being a musician!) I work on a left-hand vamp[2] in 11/8.[3] I've been at it for quite

2   A repeating rhythmic phrase
3   Eleven 8th notes to a bar

a while now and, I can play over it pretty basically. My right hand can't "think" for itself over the vamp. It can just play whatever it can play to not mess up the vamp in the left hand. I may never get "free" improvising over the vamp, but working on it continues to activate my left hand more in improvisations. The 11/8 has become a project in itself and it has been another way to get more comfortable in 11. And the counterpoint between my left and right hand is increasingly natural. This is a very new and unexplored point for most teachers and students. Practice of things that will never come to fruition but benefit overall motor skills.

Then again, long-range projects like that do sometimes come into fruition. For example, I had made a project of playing a bebop tune in 9/8.[4] It took a long time, but I eventually found myself playing in 9 without thinking. That meant 9/8 *was starting to play itself.* One night in Chicago, I was playing with my trio and I had this feeling from within, "If you want to mess around in 9/8, I think you're ready to do it in public." I decided to subject it to the ultimate test. On the third set of that night, I had a strong vodka and just called the tune. My trio would have no problem playing this tune in 9/8 because the drummer and bass player play better than I do. (Always looked for that in a trio.) If I could be tipsy, float up there and play the tune, that would mean it had joined the ranks of "things I can play in public." It did play and I had added a new ability to my tool box. You see, I won't perform anything I'm working on until it plays itself. (Pretty much the theme of the whole book.) But as stated above, I could work on things that will never mature and yet other things are improving because of it. Of course, as stated

4   Nine 8th notes to the bar

many times already, one would have to be working without the tyranny of the mind!

So, what are some guidelines for good practicing?

SMALLER IS BETTER. The fact is the less stuff you practice, the more complete your ownership of said material will be. Think of your concentration as a certain amount of water. If you put that water in a wide container, the water will be shallow. On the other hand, if you put it in a narrow container, the water will be deep. And so, it is with concentration. The smaller the example, the more you can completely master that portion.

STOP MEASURING. This is to say, don't keep focusing on the horizon. You lose appreciation for the next inch. There's nothing wrong with "a drop in the bucket." In fact, that's really the only way the bucket becomes full. Don't focus on a full bucket, rather develop an appreciation for the next drop. The great saxophonist and philosopher Wayne Shorter said, "The long road is the short road."

IF THERE'S A MISTAKE IN THERE, *LET IT HAPPEN.* Most people practice the opposite way, trying to avoid mistakes. You shouldn't try hard to play it right but *invite it to play wrong.* Then you know that if it goes right, you must have mastered it. Welcoming mistakes will fill in the gaps in your training. Those mistakes will lie in the weeds anyway waiting to sabotage you at exactly the moment you want to be perfect. So, bring on the mistakes! (When practicing!)

PRACTICE WITHOUT EGO. Think of it like brushing your teeth. You don't brush your teeth thinking "Wow! I'm really getting somewhere with this brushing. In a short time, I'll have permanently white teeth!" No. Brushing your teeth is just something that happens. No matter how well you brush them in the morning, you fully expect to brush them again that night. (If you're that good about it!) You don't measure. You simply do it. If studying was that egoless there'd be no stopping you!

NO EXPECTATIONS. Expectations ruin the moment. Haven't they always? Having no expectations in your life leads to the best results. In your practice it leads to infinite patience and a good inventory of your skills. You simply observe without the urge to weigh, measure or quantify. *Goals, yes. Dreams, yes. Expectations, NO!*

BE WILLING TO START OVER AND BE PATIENT. The missing link for many who are in a hurry to create is understanding the preparation that needs to be done for the "miracle" to happen. Embrace the idea of starting over instead of bemoaning it. "Wow, I have to start over!" Get excited about it! Everyone wants to go forward. That's their weakness. The best way to go forward is to *start over.* It's not really starting over, but rather, turning a page. A tree may grow many branches but you water it at the root. It seems counterintuitive, because the ego only wants to move forward. If you're a person who relishes starting over there's nothing you can't accomplish!

DON'T COMPARE YOURSELF TO OTHERS. The person who does all of the above can achieve any goal. There's an old saying, *compare and despair.*

The goal of practice is to remove the barriers between one's limitations and complete freedom. Look beyond functionality. Practice for *freedom.*

14 ■ The Value of Mistakes

One day I was conducting a rehearsal of some musicians for a chant we were going to play. One of the two harmonium players was unsure of the right notes. He knew what they were but they weren't readily available to him. I stopped everyone else from playing and asked him to play the chant with me, just the two of us. He made the mistake again and said, "Oops." The notes that weren't in his hands yet were clearly revealed. This phenomenon is known as a mistake. I told him that was great, that we needed to hear those mistakes, to know where they are so we would know where to focus our practicing. That being the case, "oops" is not the right word or syllable. "Ah" would be the better response. Ah, because the good news is, we've found where the mistake is! From that point on, I urged him to greet every mistake with "ah" and, if he felt that God took over his playing, he could say, "oops" for comic effect.

Sometimes I'll even say hurriedly, *"Play it wrong!"* and

the student will be surprised that they played it *completely right*. (Note: I can only fool them with this once.)

There are practical reasons mistakes have value, as well as cosmic ones. Or one could say there are *left-brain* and *right-brain* reasons for the value of mistakes. Does the perfect instrument mean one doesn't make mistakes? No, *one doesn't recoil having made them and doesn't withhold self-love because of them.* If playing right notes are blessings, then mistakes are *blessings in disguise.*

The "rightness" of all mistakes is the cosmic factor. The most common phrase is "there are no mistakes." Everybody says it but nobody believes it.

Do not fear mistakes. There are none. / Miles Davis /

Mistakes are the portals of discovery. / James Joyce /

You make your mistakes to learn how to get to the good stuff.
/ Quincy Jones /

There are only two mistakes one can make along the road to truth; not going all the way and not starting. / Buddha /
(Might or might not be his quote, but I like it.)

It is better to be high-spirited even though one makes more mistakes, than to be narrow-minded and all too prudent.
/ Vincent Van Gogh /

Anyone who has never made a mistake has never tried anything new.
and
The only way to avoid making mistakes is to have no new ideas.
/ Albert Einstein /

Freedom is not worth having if it does not include the freedom to make mistakes. / Mahatma Gandhi /

The greatest mistake you can make in life is to continually be afraid you will make one. / Elbert Hubbard /

Be not ashamed of mistakes and thus make them crimes.
/ Confucius /

I have learned throughout my life as a composer chiefly through my mistakes and pursuits of false assumptions, not by my exposure to founts of wisdom and knowledge. / Igor Stravinsky /

Without trial and error, there can be no achievement.
/ Thomas Jefferson /

I have not failed. I've just found 10,000 ways that won't work.
/ Thomas Edison /

Some of the worst mistakes of my life have been haircuts.
/ Jim Morrison /

The cosmic view of mistakes, besides the view that there are none, is that they are doorways to innovation. Of course, the biggest emotional barrier to making mistakes is the hit one takes to one's self-esteem. If we could simply skip the phase of feeling bad, we could happily encounter whatever mistakes are ready to happen. To avoid mistakes is to win the battle but lose the war. There is no true serenity in hoping not to make them. Security occurs by *inviting mistakes to happen.* That's where all the knowledge is hidden. The conscious mind is a minefield of potential mistakes. From *The Space* there are no mistakes. When they happen one is amused, rather than appalled.

I picked the quotes about mistakes that present them in the most favorable light, avoiding the quotes that call for the need for correction e.g., Dale Carnegie's famous quote, "The successful man will profit from his mistakes and try again in a different way." The value of mistakes is not just in correcting them. From *The Space,* one regards them as the way to a new freedom. It's a more exciting view. For one to approach mistakes joyfully one must make no connection between mistakes and one's sense of self-esteem. One of the greatest illusions about music is that our value is in any way related to how we play an instrument. It's understandable, but false. If the artist welcomes the mistake, it can take him to new places visually and sonically, and I suspect in other areas as well.

Herbie Hancock describes the perfect example of this cosmic principle in the first chapter of his book, *Possibilities.* (I usually read the first chapter of most books!) He describes a gig the Miles Davis quintet was playing in Stockholm, Sweden. The band was really heating up on the tune "So What?" and the whole thing is building up to Miles' solo. Herbie writes, "Miles starts playing his solo, and just as he's about to really let loose, he takes a breath. And right then I play a chord that is just so wrong. I don't even know where it came from—it's the wrong chord, in the wrong place and now it's hanging out there like a piece of rotten fruit. I think, *Oh, shit.* It's as if we've all been building this gorgeous house of sound, and I just accidentally put a match to it. Miles pauses for a fraction of a second, and then plays some notes that somehow, miraculously make my chord sound right. In that moment I believe my mouth actually fell open. What kind of alchemy was this? And then Miles took off from there, unleashing a solo that took the song in a new direction."[1]

Yeah! That's what I'm talking about! Some people like things for different reasons. People like jazz because it is (or was) entertaining, because it has (or had) a beat, or they may be enamored with the sociology, or believe that jazz has a political purpose—"America's only original art form," and such. For me, it is this cosmic principle that I've always loved about jazz. You break the rules and you may get to *new music!* It's not a cop out because usually it's the masters *of* the rules that get to *break them.*

I once heard a story about Charlie Parker. For those of you who don't know who he is, he was one of the founders of the style of jazz in the '40s called *Bebop.* Charlie Parker was a master, innovator and virtuoso in every way. He was referred to as *Bird.* Sometimes on the road he would travel alone and play with local bands, saving the money or just making more of it. The way I heard it, there was a pianist who was in the band and it was his job to pick up Bird every night from the hotel, take him to the gig and after the gig, take him back. He said that in the several weeks Bird was there he never said a word to him. Each night he got in the car, got out of the car, played the gig, got in the car, got out and back into the hotel, saying nothing to the piano player. This went on for weeks. One night on the bandstand, the piano player spaced out and played a completely wrong chord, just like Herbie did with Miles. He said Bird turned towards him and said, *"I hear you."*

I think no jazz musician embodies this spirit, this reality more than Thelonious Monk. Another acknowledged genius

1   *Possibilities,* Herbie Hancock

and also a co-founder of Bebop; his compositions defied all conventional wisdom. He took chord progressions that had been thought to be old and corny and made them hip in a new way. His melodies are such strong statements of his personality that it's hard for any other musicians to play a Monk composition *without trying to sound like Monk!* As a pianist, Monk's freedom to make mistakes was so persuasive that when people play like him, *they think it's cool to make the same mistakes*, like it was part of that style of music. And when I call them mistakes, I'm referring to missed notes, chords that border on cluster, rhythms that are so far out yet somehow work.

I always imagined a musicologist teaching his class at Columbia in the daytime and telling his students what notes were unacceptable, then going to the Village Vanguard that night and hearing Monk play those exact notes and freaking out because *they had suddenly become the new right notes.* In fact, he might have had an experience hearing those "mistakes," which he had never had hearing the "correct notes." This is what makes hip people hip. The hippest characters in movies are the ones who aren't afraid to go against convention, society or "the system."

Now I'll tell a story of my own. I used to teach at a master class/retreat/ music camp—whatever you call—it in Sandpoint, Idaho. It was headed by Gunther Schuller, one of the great conductors and composers of our time. He was also a wonderful French horn player. Although Gunther was a master classical musician and composer, he dearly loved jazz. He was involved in many historic jazz projects and not nearly recognized enough for the incredible jazz composer and arranger he was. Since he had his feet firmly planted in the main stream of both worlds, jazz and classical, his idea was that jazz musicians would be well trained enough to deal with difficult classical-type material and that classical musicians would learn to improvise like the jazz guys. He called it *Third Stream*. His camp then had jazz and classical players training alongside each other. The jazz students would attend the recitals and orchestra concerts and the classical students would come to our gigs and the jam session every night.

The following is a story with two morals. One is the power of mistakes and the other is the power of detachment. One day the violin teacher at the camp, Young-Nam Kim, a great violinist, asked me to join him on a piece at one of the recitals. It was the Brahms D minor for string trio and piano, third movement. I hadn't played a classical piece since college and I had never performed one, and certainly not with virtuosos like these. There was a real possibility I could make a fool of myself so I said, *"Sure, why not?"*

I didn't have much time to practice because I was mainly there to teach, but my family was also with me. I knew they didn't want to hear about my working on this piece in my spare time. We had very few rehearsals. The night before the concert, Gunther wanted to hear how the piece was coming. I wasn't prepared enough but I was also very attached to impressing him. I flipped and flopped around the piece until mercifully, we were done. It was an obvious disaster. Gunther just said, almost to himself, "Well, you'll play this tomorrow and then it will be over." Boy, that sank me.

I realized that I had completely abandoned my own principles of *Effortless Mastery*. The next day I decided to surrender the performance, to practice totally from *The Space* and let the chips fall where they may. To do that, I had to let my hands play every note *very* slowly. I did this while being in the one-pointed focus of my own inner space. The other players were in different corners of the room practicing certain passages furiously. One by one, they came over to the piano and just looked. I looked at them and said, "What?"

Young Nam said, "Ooh, you practice so *good!*"

I said, "thanks," but figured, *so what?* Now I was in *The Space.*

The time came to perform. We started the piece and my hands went, almost on their own, to the right notes. There were passages my hands had not yet owned, usually involving the left hand. (Most jazz pianists have a more developed right hand than left.) But I was so loose that whenever my left hand wasn't ready, it just slipped away for a moment, or played a reduced version of its part. The point was, *I was keeping the groove,* so as a group we were cruising along fine. After a bit, I realized that that slow practice had somehow enhanced my memory of the piece. I began to look up, away from the sheet music and smile at Young Nam. I do this at jazz gigs, I laugh and smile with whomever I'm playing with. A few people in the audience started to laugh. They weren't used to seeing someone that loose in a classical group. Young Nam looked up to see what people were laughing at and saw me smiling at him. He broke into a broad grin and a cheer went up in the audience! We were burning ahead with the piece and at the end we got a standing ovation.

Afterward, jazz and classical musicians were coming up to me, thrilled with what we played. And remember, by classical standards, *I played awful.* But the spirit of the moment seemed to be much more important to all who were there— except one! The local piano teacher shimmied up to me like a cartoon character, tapped me on the shoulder and said, "Young man, sloppy Brahms," just like that, and sauntered away. Well, everyone was angry with her. How could she say that? It was so fun to listen to. I just said, "Yep, you're right." I didn't mind at all. The piece was nothing if not sloppy! I just didn't care and no one else seemed to either. Gunther came up to me and said, "That's what I've been going for all these years with *Third Stream*. I loved it!"

When I was attached to him liking my performance, I played terribly and now that I was detached, I got the comments my ego would have liked all along. I had to dissolve my ego while playing in order to get the response my ego would have so desired! You see, there's a lesson here in embracing mistakes. As I celebrated them, they became stimulating to the audience. The other lesson is in detachment. By letting go of how good I played the piece, I was windsurfing through the thing!

In practicing, mistakes aren't things to be avoided; they're to be attracted. Like a vacuum cleaner looks for dust to scoop up, you want to be a vacuum for mistakes, you're looking to make them. And when you find one, say, "AH!" Enjoy them! In performance, enjoy your mistakes and you won't make any. Or the mistakes will be more delightful than the correct notes! We want to approach the instrument with complete detachment every time: "Oh look, suddenly I'm playing. How about that?" When we do that, we return to the instrument without care and we find out *exactly where the mistakes lie*. Then we know exactly what elements to practice.

As stated before, if we hide the mistakes from ourselves because we don't want to feel bad, or we don't want to be confronted with having to start over or go back over something, *then we win the battle but lose the war*. We manage to get through that particular piece without mistakes, but we lose the opportunity to make the piece and our overall playing stronger, more secure. Solving problems in a piece, solving them for real means elevating our game. No mistakes, no feedback. No finding an effective way to erase the mistake and the faulty muscle memory that created it. Playing it correctly sometimes is an outer change that is temporary, for if conditions are not right, e.g., we're nervous, didn't get a good night's sleep, or we have a cold, we make the mistake. Confronting the mistake as evidence that *we need more training* moves us towards mastery. If we're not hobbled by emotion, we can gain that insight. One who has to manage their body so they don't make a mistake is the very definition of mediocrity. Lose the fear of mistakes and *celebrate!*

15 ■ Notes on Patience

Patience 1

The reason adults don't usually improve is because they have the patience of an adult. A child can work on something for a long time and, since he's never been there before, accept it as his daily homework, but by the time he is an adult, he wants everything to improve by yesterday. As the reality of real-time progress sets in, he either gets bored or discouraged before he reaches the goal.

Patience 2

This is the secret, dear one: do your daily portion of work and move on with your day. Treat it as something accomplished that is "better than nothing." After all, what are the chances of improving without any practice?

(I'm writing a book on exercise. It is called, *Better Than Nothing! Lol*)

Patience 3

Boredom comes from the expectations of progress not being met. Therefore, drop expectations. Just do your little portion of work with self-love and devotion. Increase the amount of devotion you can muster over time. You will soon be lifted from the impatience for progress, and content in the sweetness of action.

Patience 4

A farmer, after planting the seeds for his various crops, is not concerned when the crops will be ready to harvest, because he is knowledgeable in the nature of such things; he knows exactly what month he will harvest that crop, barring extenuating circumstances such as weather. Worry never causes him to go out to the fields in the middle of the night to tug on the shoots. Secure in his knowledge, he spends all his time and effort doing the things he knows will help the crop grow, never doubting the time frame. We know how long it takes for a flower to grow, but we have no idea how long it takes for a new habit to grow in ourselves. Adding to our frustration, we usually underestimate the time it takes for actions to take root and flower. It is for this reason that we usually give up on actions before we can harvest results.

Patience 5

We are much more knowledgeable about outer nature than inner nature. We know that the sun is always in the sky during the day, no matter how many clouds block its brilliance. The sky might be dark at 2 p.m. because of thick clouds, but we never doubt that there's a sun behind them, shining as brightly as ever and not diminished in any way. But on an emotionally dark day, we doubt the existence of that light within ourselves, and certainly of its brilliance.

Patience 6

Have patience dear one, the sun always rises, but it does so in its own time. Your practice will bear fruit. It is unavoidable—IF—and this is a big if, you never cease to take the action until the result has been realized.

Patience 7

Confucius actually said, "Study as if you were following someone you could not overtake."

Patience 8

Suppose you practiced harmonizing one note with another, creating a chord progression of two chords. Imagine if you did one variation after another, day after day, for twenty years. Imagine it became a habit like reading the paper. Do you think you could avoid becoming a master of **harmony**?

Patience 9

Imagine practicing one, four-note pattern, perfecting it, and connecting it to another four-note pattern, forming a perfect eight-note line. Imagine doing one of those a day for twenty years. Imagine it became a hobby like doing the crossword puzzle. Do you think you could avoid becoming a master of **melody**?

Patience 10

Suppose you practiced one rhythmic phrase after another, never moving on until the previous one was absolutely mastered. Suppose you patiently did this for ten years. Do you think you could avoid becoming a master of **rhythm**?

Patience 11

Think about the way one does a book of crossword puzzles. Does this person say, "I've got to get these puzzles done as fast as possible so I can move on to the next set of games. I wonder if I'm getting better at crossword puzzles? Am I getting better yet?"

No, of course not. They are just recreational content to pass the time. They probably hope that they don't finish them too fast so that they will remain occupied. They don't burden themselves with the question of where are they going. They enjoy the moment.

16 ■ Meditation #2

Close your eyes. Go away. Let everything completely leave you. Leave everything behind. Now enjoy the tension and release of your in-breath and out-breath. Become the shell. An empty shell. It's a strong shell, a sturdy shell, very still and empty. You can almost hear an echo in the place, like in an empty warehouse.

Now, center on the sound of the breath going in and going out. Enjoy the slight contraction of the inhale, and the release of the exhale. Imagine a machine that only did that. What if the sound of the air going in and out was as satisfying as the sound of the waves of the ocean? What if you were forever content just to ride that sound with your awareness? You would never want for anything again. You'd be empty of all other sounds, thoughts, desires, and needs. Perhaps you would occasionally require food, water, sleep, and waste elimination. But imagine a building like that, an edifice whose walls are sturdy and large, but *The Space* inside is empty and cavernous. There is one machine in it, a breathing machine. The only sound filling the huge hall is the oceanic sound of breath "rushing in and releasing outward."

That's really the whole meditation. But hey, your eyes are closed and you are listening, so I'll elucidate quietly under the silence. Let's imagine the benefits. If one were truly as empty as a vacant warehouse, if one's walls were that sturdy and if the simple sound of your inhale and exhale filled the shell's awareness, you wouldn't want or need anything, but you would be a space for things to enter. Everyone needs extra space, right?

Grace, for example, if that concept works for you. Instead of praying for Grace, you would be a *magnet* for Grace! I'm sure God's got too much of it—Grace that is. He'd probably appreciate the extra storage space—a place to store His grace, His blessings, and His abundance. Maybe it's musical ideas you crave. When you empty yourself completely and allow Musical Grace to fill you, wonders may occur! What about love? Empty of the need to be loved you may *become love*. Oh yeah, let's do this!

Imagine love filling the eyes and ears, the nose and cranium, the neck and shoulders, the arms and hands. Love running like a river down a mountain, filling the chest, the stomach, the hips, and then, at the fork, becoming two streams, the right and left leg. Love running down the thighs, the knees, into the calves, ankles and feet. Imagine the toes swelling with *liquid love*. The fingers being filled like tiny water balloons with *love, or music, or God. Whatever you'd most desire to be filled with.* That's it.

Commentary

We have a barn right now at our house that's filled with all kinds of stuff we can't fit in the house. Old bags (or old baggage perhaps?), outdoor furniture, out-of-date electronic

music equipment, (wa-wa pedal, anyone?), wood, and tons
of boxes of memories we'll probably never revisit again.
I would so love to empty that barn, insulate it, and fill the
first floor with my beautiful piano, recording equipment,
my beautiful desk for my computer, speakers, and whatever
comprises my studio. In the upstairs, I'd love to put another
desk, filing cabinets, nice furniture, comfy couches, and re-
clining chairs. Oh, and recliners on the first floor too. Every
square inch of *The Space* would then be dedicated to my
comfort, my pleasure (forgot to mention the 60" monitor
screen!), my art, my craft, and let's even throw in a portable gym to improve my physical well-being. A spot would
also be kept empty, clean, and lit with candles. There
I would set up my *puja* for spiritual practice and worship.
I definitely need that space as well. That's the space where
I spend time with my right brain, emptying and allowing
higher forces to take over and use me to do the rest of the
things I could be doing in that barn. That's my fantasy.
Perhaps we'll get there. But for now, let's just appreciate the
metaphor.

OK, back to the meditation . . .

If your space was empty, if you were comfortable, even
content with emptiness, the things you could attract into
that space! If your mind was always content to listen to the
rise and fall of the air machine that expands and contracts
endlessly, if that sensual movement were enough for your
awareness to feast on, every subtle idea would have your full
attention when it appeared.

Commentary

When I get filled with thoughts and desires, I get over-
stuffed like after Thanksgiving dinner. There are too many

ideas, too many possibilities and therefore, too many problems. I'm stuck on the couch again and will medicate and numb out with social media or Netflix. So right now, let's shut down the three devices or the five apps we have open simultaneously, and go back to that cavernous, open, empty space. The empty body, the empty mind.

Back to the meditation . . .

As it is said in the first step, *drop your hands and go back to The Space.* That is always a great new starting point to imbibe a whole new batch of blessings. Miraculously, after all the electrifying ideas you received, you are empty again and just as attractive to new ideas and actions. If it becomes an instinctive action to stop, go back to *The Space* and become empty every time. Your warehouse will become filled with an amazing life. In reality, this breathing is going on without your awareness, let alone *gratitude.* It's the one thing that if stopped, you wouldn't care about anything else.

Can we do it? It takes practice to stop whenever you become aware that you're straining at the edges to contain ambition and action. If you feel tension from the plethora of too many ideas at once, too many *desires* at once, and if it all seems overwhelming at any point, become aware of it and close your eyes. Count or just watch your breaths and become empty. At least, make your best attempt. The more automatic that becomes, the less you will feel stifled, blocked, despairing, and a whole host of negative emotions and feelings that we are so well aware of. We're so used to those settings that we think they're the only reality. It doesn't have to be that way. You want to introduce this new move into your life-rhythm and repeat it again and again.

What a magnet you become for new ideas, electrifying music, or the incentive to take bold actions!

Once more, let us again *go away*. Disappear and leave everything behind. Become empty. Now detect that little breathing generator, producing the lovely sounds of inhale and exhale. Our *inner massage* coming from the sensual *stretch* of our inhale and *release* of our exhale. Mmmm . . . sooo . . . gooood. . . . Become comfortable, even content, even *grateful f*or that! Everything added unto you will be a gift.

Drop your hands, *drop your demands,*
go into The Space . . . and become empty.

17 ■ Improvisation
Unlocking its secrets

Improvisation presents itself moment-to-moment and you must be ready to receive it. If called upon to improvise, you trust it. It is like receiving the impulses that form your life. Improvisation isn't a distraction. It emerges out of an ocean of impulses. Evidently, it's a different part of the brain being activated, because if you ask a classical musician to improvise, they will act like you just told them to jump off a cliff or into a void. Indeed, it is a void because they have not connected with the part of their brain where improvisation occurs. Most people aren't attuned to that flow. We're much more focused on the sobering thoughts of success or survival. Sometimes we get a cool wind from the north, an impulse that seems too good to be true. Yet we are afraid to follow because we might look foolish or make a wrong choice. Maybe we won't feel safe. Honoring that voice and embracing wherever it takes us is a courageous form of improvisation.

But for many that corridor has yet to be opened. There is a flow to improvisation and what stunts you is the fear of where it's taking you. To improvise, one has to trust decisions or musical note choices as they come, the right ones *and wrong ones.* Improvisation isn't developed by knowing the right notes to choose or the right moves to make. It develops from following intuition *whether it's right or wrong.* Once the channel to that flow is opened, we can integrate knowledge. But even knowledgeable people may be afraid to improvise. The channel must be opened. Trust is a habit. For the musician, that means developing the consciousness and willingness to move from note to note, even if one hasn't the *language to do so.* Hence, *bad playing and bad decision-making is irrelevant to the issue of improvisation.*

Before one is challenged to improvise on a particular skill, or with a particular language, it is beneficial to experience improvisation in the raw, so to speak. Raw movement, raw sound, raw action, the swing of the arms with a golf club in hand, dancing, singing, or using a paintbrush or pen. You connect with the movement itself, honoring it, or pretending it's absolutely the perfect movement of the universe. You *pretend* you are making the most beautiful sound regardless of what that sound is. Cultivating this belief is more important than proving its validity.

Love every move. The optimum flow of ideas, even the greatest potential for brilliance, is to accept with love every impulse that travels through you. Most of us can't do that, but we can practice it in the abstract. Again, let's play with the idea of emptying ourselves completely. Emptying ourselves of what? In the case of moving or dancing, it might be caring how foolish we look. Broadly speaking, it means emptying oneself of ego. Going into *The Space* means becoming empty. (Step 2)

Let's try improvising with our bodies. First, let's go into *The Space* as much as we're willing or able to. Don't worry if you think your space is not perfect. Thinking you're not perfect is just that, a thought. Isn't that one of the subtle ways we sabotage ourselves? I wonder if a tree thinks it's perfect? Or, for our purpose, imagine that you're going into *The Space perfectly*. You can use meditation #2 from the previous chapter, or any means you're familiar with, or, *just go into The Space.*

From that space, move an arm, a leg, a finger, anything. Turn your head clockwise or counterclockwise. The movement is irrelevant. The point is, from *The Space imagine someone or something else is doing it.* You could imagine you were a puppet or some kind of inanimate object that doesn't move unless someone else moves it. Here you must use your imagination. This use of the imagination helps to stimulate creativity.

As you move, imagine your body is moving by itself. If you have an instrument, you could play a note on that instrument, *but imagine you're not doing anything. Someone or something is playing that note, making that move through you.* Now, as soon as you lose that feeling, *stop!* Really. Stop what you're doing and drop the movement. Return to following your breathing. If you've lost patience for the exercise, forget it, take a break, or try it again when you're more willing. But if you're still in it, then *move.*

I have an idea: I'm discovering an exercise that you're reading as I'm discovering it. *That's the magic of improvisation.* I have enough confidence in what I receive to commit to it right here and now without ever having tried it, but I know it works because *improvisation works!*

> Feel energy in your hand. Imagine you had no way to move it, but you feel a buzzing energy gathering in the hand. Come on . . . Forget if it's happening or not. Stop being an adult. *Pretend* you have no control over it and some mystical energy is gathering in the hand. (You can even use the soundtrack from a Harry Potter movie!) Let your hand float while you watch it, *as if it were someone else's hand.* Perhaps it wants to travel. Follow it as it goes around the room. You may have to get up because the hand wants to move around the room. Feel like you are following it wherever it wants to go. Keep staring at the hand. Stare at it in wonder, like, *"What's happening here?"* Stare at nothing but the hand and follow its movement wherever it goes. If you lose this awareness, or start to think about it, *drop your hand and go back into The Space.* If you have moved from your chair, go back to your chair, sit down and take a break. If you think you've had enough, then go pay a bill or something. Do it as long as you're interested, willing, or patient enough to do it.

Before you begin improvising, you tune into the center of your being, whatever that means to you. This is about improvisation and everything in the book so far has led to this exercise. Whatever moves you from your left brain to your right, your individual mind to the Universal Mind; if God is your God; then let him move you. Whatever it is that is larger than you, *become empty and let it fill you, then move.*

Letting the higher power fill you is a spiritual/psychological exercise. What you do next while remaining aware of that space *is improvisation.*

In order for one to improvise, one must be able to trust the movement. It is even more delicious if one *loves every movement, eliminating all other possibilities.* This is true of performance of any kind: planned, written or improvised. At the time of performance of the act, there is no time to judge the action. There certainly is no time to amend the action. It doesn't help one's performance to *wish they performed the action better than they do.* No, there is only time to *accept the action,* if possible, *with love.* The time for fixing things is long gone. Practice is how we prepare for intelligent action when it's time to perform, time to act. The thing that makes our performance flow is embracing whatever is available. In an improvised performance, *there's no time to look, only to find,* and wherever you find yourself, *there you are!* Abundance, compassion, and brilliance can be studied through the mystical process of improvisation: ***jazz.***

Let's change the meaning of the word:

JAZZ = TRANSFORMATION

As stated before, opening the channel to improvisation is best done in the abstract. One must be comfortable with movement, sound, color or data, whatever the materials are of his art/craft. Then one may channel raw intuition into intelligent forms. Imagine the pure light of consciousness manifesting through a filter of expertise. The work is precise, but powered by that light. That is the stuff of genius. Receiving the divine light on one end, and letting it power intelligent actions on the other, is the game of music and the game of life, the game of *mastery.* It's also about becoming familiar with the improvisor in you, and allowing it to manifest when you hit a wall in your thinking or problem solving.

One technique is practicing flight without flight patterns. Choices made by intuition rather than fear of consequences.

This kind of free experimentation gives you a personal relationship with the tools and textures of your trade. You connect to what movements or decisions feel like, what splashes of color look like, and what swaths of notes sound like. Self-love is part of the practice, with or without reason to self-love. It illuminates the experiment, if you can conjure it. That is a love that literally IS *unconditional*. One learns self-trust, *trusting your gut*, as it were.

Hopefully in the future, I envision having Effortless Mastery retreats. A safe place to be foolish and trust the *improvisor* in you.

An early example of this in my life was when my father taught me to drive. I swear, this is the hippest thing he ever did for me! He had me drive to an empty parking lot at a Waldbaum's supermarket. (This is back when stores were actually closed on Sundays!) Then he got out of the car and told me to just drive around. There were no boundaries, no cement blocks or metal poles, nothing to hit. He told me to floor the gas pedal, do figure eights, wheelies, anything I wanted to. Wow! It was like a ride in an amusement park. I sped, braked hard, soft, turning the wheel this way and that. When I was done, I drove back to where my father was waiting for me. He didn't even explain what the benefit of that would be. But driving home, *I had 100 percent more control of the wheel, the brakes, and driving the car.* I advanced so fast in mastering the car, because of *irresponsible and failure-free experimentation!*

Put your hands on the piano and just start playing notes. Any notes. Now you're improvising. That's all there is to it. Use your elbows and hit the keys; you're improvising. Kids use it and *adults lose it.*

One the other hand, while improvising on chords one

may not feel so free because one may not be comfortable with chords. In that case, a lack of expertise causes the lack of freedom. Improvisation is opening that channel of the brain, then one may expound through the filter of one's training; sort of the left-brain, right-brain subject covered earlier.

I have a friend and advisor to the Effortless Mastery Institute named Rob Fried. He was Head of Global Sales at Bridgewater Associates, one of the biggest investment management firms in the world. He described examples of improvisation in his business:

"Improv skills would be any choice that is made in the game that was not part of the original plan or format, that arises due to a change in the context. For example, if the key decision maker comes to the meeting 10 minutes late, an improv skill would be acknowledging him and doing a quick recap before continuing the meeting. Another improv skill would be the choice to use humor, or have a more personal introduction, to establish rapport and give the meeting a warmer feeling than many business meetings typically have. Another improv skill is to tack in a direction that was not planned, based on questions that are asked, or new information that is learned in the introduction. If someone says what the biggest problem on their mind is, and it wasn't something you knew or heard before, a smart play would be to address that question instead of pursuing what was originally planned, but only if the quality of the conversation can be high."

Perhaps the practice of embracing Rob's own intuition and impulses made him more resourceful and flexible. (He too is a musician!)

Freedom in form means mastery of the form, and a will-

ingness to be free. Rules may have indeed been made to be broken but *one must really know the rules to break them!* (Schoenberg[1] comes to mind!)

Intelligent improvisation would be the freedom I felt in the parking lot wedded to the skill of a race car driver. This is where freedom, muscle memory, left/right-brain integration, individual and Universal mind merge to create the perfect instrument. Mastery of skills have been absorbed to the point of effortlessness.

On the piano, all the white keys constitute either a C major or A minor scale. That's why people find themselves making a bit of sense on the piano before they have any idea what they're doing. The white keys alone suggest intelligent design. (No pun intended.)

However, if that person wishes to create the same major/ minor improv in, say, Eb—that would be impossible unless they knew the Eb and C minor scales. Now, if they kinda sorta knew the Eb scale, they still wouldn't experience anywhere near the freedom they felt when they played on all the white keys. But if they *mastered* the Eb scale, with its combination of black and white notes, to the point of effortless mastery, they would feel just as free improvising in Eb as they did in C.

Inspired improvisation backed up with mastery of notes, skills, facts, details—anything—has led to profound results in music, enormous strides in research. In a certain scenario, two people are experts; one is also a fearless improviser.

---

1   1874-1951-an Austrian-born composer, music theorist, teacher, writer, and painter. He is widely considered one of the most influential composers of the 20th century. He was associated with the expressionist movement in German poetry and art, and leader of the Second Viennese School. As a Jewish composer, Schoenberg was targeted by the Nazi Party, which labeled his works as degenerate music and forbade them from being published.

He is the one that breaks new ground. One has to be in possession of both qualities.

————

There's music composition software called Finale. I've used it since 1996. Another year I was teaching at that music camp in Sandpoint I mentioned before. I was also writing music for a jazz orchestra gig I had coming up. I brought my wife and five-year-old daughter Katheryn so they could also enjoy the place. The camp was in the mountains. Looking out our windows, I was astounded at how big the sky was. We were high enough to feel level with the clouds.

With Finale software, there is a feature where you can hit the caps lock and a number, and then every note you touched on the keyboard would appear in the score with the value of that number. Normally, you had to hit a note on the keyboard and a number on the computer, but with the caps lock on, all you had to do is hit the (piano) keyboard. All notes have the same value. You could smash the notes anywhere and they would appear on your score. I asked my daughter to just hit the keys anywhere she wanted, like a child would normally do with a piano keyboard. Of course, I wanted to think it was brilliant, but it was just a bunch of notes. After she was done, I merely started to play with them. I did variation after variation without any particular goal and eventually this piece organized itself into a symphony. I called it Symphony In The Clouds. It was wonderfully, wild yet wonderfully organized. It could not have been achieved any other way.

Another time, I was in my studio just playing drums. There was a bass drum pattern I found interesting. Then I had an impulse to write a piece off of nothing but that bass drum pattern. For those of you who don't know, one could hardly write a piece on less. I gave the bass drum pattern to the bass trombone. They were literally the first notes of the piece. I kept doing things with this pattern, seemingly with no direction or aim. Sometime into the piece I had the funny idea (impulse) of quoting a bit of the melody of the old pop song, *The House of the Rising Sun.* It was a similar feeling to driving around that parking lot. It was like, "Who cares? What could possibly go wrong?" It was an impulse and I followed it without hesitation. I kept writing stuff without care and again, in another form, this melody to "The House of the Rising Sun" came up. I was 50 percent into a piece that had no aim and I was suddenly thrilled with this proposition: "Could this actually *be* an arrangement of *The House of The Rising Sun?* What turned me on was that much of the arrangement had nothing to do with that song! Both these compositions remain among the most original and exciting pieces I've ever written.[2]

Some composers create something with a lot of control, and then they try to create the "illusion" of chaos. I start with chaos (irresponsible writing, *reckless driving!)* and I keep removing things until it sounds ordered. Hopefully, it shows you how to get to high creative ground through that "other doorway."

Forging ahead with concentration, but also with fearlessness and imagination, being willing to throw it all away and waste one's time, it's all wonderful parameters of the human mind and the guiding light of improvisation.

---

2   Can be heard on the *Institute of Higher Learning* with the Brussels Jazz Orchestra.

18 ■ Turning Yourself On

I've coached musicians to touch their instrument without expectation, which is where fear comes from. Playing notes without judgment, how do they process the sound they hear? They have to learn to brainwash themselves to love the sound they make, and not wait until they hear a sound they would like to love. (The song says, *"If you can't be . . . with the (sound) you love . . . love the (sound) you're with . . .)*[1] Looking for a sound you will love is like a dog chasing its own tail. Instead, whatever sound you make, pretend you love that sound until you vibrate with it. In fact, this is probably how music has progressed harmonically through its history. An inspired musician eschewing the conventional rules of the day in favor of the stronger urge to *get off!*

Playing music is essentially an act of turning yourself on. If you're not making that connection, what's the point? It's not exactly the most brilliant career choice! It only makes sense and is more likely if one is addicted to it, addicted to

1   Crosby, Stills, Nash & Young

the feel, the sound, etc. It's no accident the most powerful performers were often drug addicts or alcoholics because the strongest motivation for their art is to get off, get high, not just simply doing good work. Doing good work is what artists say after the fact, but the actual work is led by their desire to *get off*. That *leads* them to certain places. The desire to do something well is not the true power. Not for artists/addicts.

I liken it to a light bulb. A light bulb has a filament and when you turn the electricity on, it courses through that filament and starts to vibrate and the room fills with light. The filament doesn't light the room by hoping it can generate light or having the desire or obligation to do so. A current from a *greater power source* courses through the lightbulb, causing it to vibrate at such a high frequency that the room is lit. The urge to feel *that buzz*, that vibration, governs so much of the choices a true addict or true artist makes. It's just a fact that many have been "Looking For Buzz In All the Wrong Places." *(Another old song!)* When the artist starts to vibrate, the audience feels the buzz. If the performer's soul vibrates, the other souls in the room start to vibrate. Just like on a suburban street, when one dog barks they all bark. I believe that's the real fascination with art. Behind the façade of entertainment, it's really *about people seeking the light, like moths drawn to the flame.*

With this different understanding one can also realize *music is fun*. If you're not having fun, if music doesn't enhance your joy in this lifetime, you're making too big a deal out of it. But the same is true of sadness. If joy is not your engine but sadness or depression is, then it is the *salvation* of music you crave. In either case, it is based on the solid foundation of *craving*.

Of all the arts, music is the only one in which the verb to

commit the act is *play*. That should tell us something. Music only makes sense when it inspires us to play, to sorrow, to action, or to love. We play right notes, wrong notes, consonant or dissonant notes; we play fast, slow, soft, loud, gently or angry, if that's what the body and mind need to experience at that time. The musician who plays music with caution has no aura. But when the music expresses inspiration, hate, lust, spirit, or whatever, that player resonates and then the audience resonates. They all radiate, and that radiation lights a room. The God of music hath proclaimed, *"Let there be light."* When one has transcended the conventions of art and has elevated to *getting off*, the art becomes the spirit food other humans need to enhance their lives. In ancient India's spiritual texts, the emphasis is on intoxication, not punishment. That's what sent me east. Some of the most spiritual people may be the most vulnerable to addiction. The need to vibrate is overriding and must be satisfied. For some, that need is filled when they meet their guru. Others, perhaps when they consider themselves "born again."

Addicts have traditionally been the most powerful communicators. They're not trying to satisfy us, or some imaginary aesthetic, or save the world for that matter. *They're just trying to get off!* Selfish, you say? Picasso was selfish, and incidentally, *changed the world!* That's the way an artist can lift up his brethren, by **turning himself on.**

I will now apply my limited knowledge and erudition to music history. Mozart wanted to write operas in German, operas the common people could enjoy. The language of the day was Italian, and the subjects of art tended to be the triumph of morality or religiosity. I think I can imagine the conversation.

"Herr Mozart, we will commission you to write an opera.

Of course, we expect it to be written and sung in Italian. Will you do it?"

Mozart scratches his face a little and then his underarms (one member of the court swore he saw Mozart smelling his fingers!) and said, "Man, don't lay that on me! I can't get off in Italian. Ah needs ma German, you dig?" There it was, innovation born, not out of the desire to innovate, but the *need* for something different.

There is an old worn out saying, "Necessity is the mother of invention." I would say in art, *boredom is the mother of invention.* Shakespeare, I dare say, probably did the same thing. He was the first to write poems and plays for commoners as well as royalty. These foundational figures in all of Western music and literature *were likely two guys getting off!*

People often ask me how I got the touch and the sound I have on the piano. They expect an answer that has to do with something physical. There are techniques that purportedly improve one's touch and sound. They may be effective, I don't know. But I have never put my arms in a certain position, moved my elbows, straightened my back, rotated my wrists, flapped my wings or clucked like a chicken! I simply *enjoy* the pushing of the buttons. When you were a child and you got into an elevator with your parents, what's the first thing you wanted to do? *Push the buttons!* You wanted to push every button to every floor, several times if possible. If you like the feeling of pressing the keys, you're halfway towards getting a nice sound.

Well, that's what it still feels like to me. *I like to push the buttons.* Sensuality can compensate for a world of technique. At universities, one can't use all of one's devices to illustrate a point in the age of extreme appropriateness. But I can give two salacious samples.

1 What part of your lover do you most like to touch? You are *drawn* to touch that part—can't wait to *get off* touching that part? Ever had to think about touching it correctly? That's what an instrument can feel like.

2 A good improvised solo is akin to masturbation. You start moving fast, slow, up, down, hard, soft, all the time being led by an *inexorable* feeling, coming to an *undeniable* climax or, if you like, a *resolution*.

Once I had a student, a woman, who could play the piano pretty well but the notes were always stiff and sounded brittle. She believed in my philosophy 100 percent and studied with me in earnest for quite a while. But she just couldn't let go when she played the piano. I didn't see any evidence of this nervousness or stiffness in her as a person. I enjoyed her company. But when she sat down to that piano, it was a different story. By taking her through the first step, she would find that sensual *contact point* sometimes. One might call it the *sweet spot* between finger and key. But she would easily lose it and would need constant reinforcement. This is not surprising and I had empathy for her blockage, as I have had that experience in other areas of life. You change and then you change back. I have compassion for those who experience it in music.

One day, I was in the town she lived in and gave her a lesson in her apartment. She was a real horse lover, and animal lover in general. She had a big fuzzy dog in her apartment. I don't know the breed; to me it was just big and cuddly. We were at the piano working on easing into *The Space* again when we took a break. She went over to her dog and really gave it love. She petted it with such love and obvious enjoyment. Her whole demeanor changed. There was so much *grace* in the way she petted and patted her dog. I said, "Wait a minute, see what you're feeling and doing right now? Stay in that space and come over to the piano." She went over and then I said, "Now keep petting your dog. Keep thinking of the joy you get from touching him. Drop the fingers but keep thinking about the dog." Well, it happened! It all happened! Suddenly the movement was different: the demeanor, the touch and yes, the sound! When she thought about playing piano, she got stiff and afraid. When she thought of petting her dog, her touch became sensual, even *spiritual*.

Miles Davis and Frank Sinatra

Many people think that you have to be a stellar talent on an instrument to be worthy. In fact, virtuosity is not the most important element. *Inner turn-on* is. Miles Davis was not even close to the best trumpet player of his day. He came to prominence following a true virtuoso, Dizzy Gillespie. If it were baseball, it would be like following a home run hitter with a Punch and Judy" hitter. Miles hung in there, but didn't flourish like his predecessor. The tempos of the Bebop era were fast, the chords going by with lightning speed. Miles was able to hold on, but wasn't nearly as comfortable as Dizzy.

But after playing with Charlie Parker, Miles looked *inside*. He found his voice. He vibed with it and it kept him company. All other details, styles, customs, faded into the background. He found his chords and his tempo, and he melded with them and you know what happened? *Birth of the Cool.*[2]

As I said, if we rated jazz trumpet players of the 20th century on the merits of their trumpet playing, I'm not even sure he would break the top ten, *yet it was entirely Miles Davis's century.* It wouldn't be until the dawning of the 21st century that young trumpet players would stop imitating him, *even making the same mistakes!* Some still imitate him to this day. In fact, one didn't really think only of trumpet when thinking about Miles Davis, there was too much music there.

Frank Sinatra is another case in point. Thinking about the other singers of his day, I remember Dick Haymes, in particular. Haymes was better looking and had a better voice. He made a few movies, most notably *One Touch of Venus.* He was like a clean cut, all-American version of Frank Sinatra. In fact, it was Frank himself who introduced Haymes as his replacement for the Tommy Dorsey band. Haymes had a great career with many hit records, but does anyone under eighty remember him?

The fact is, Frank Sinatra connected with a *pleasure spot deep inside himself.* When he sang, it actually hit the pleasure spot of his audience. He had a deep need to be loved. That can also power a performance, as was the case with Judy Garland. There were many other male crooners of the time— Vic Damone, Perry Como, Vaughn Monroe, and on and on. Can anyone deny that the 20th century belonged entirely to Frank Sinatra? Today it's almost like a cult. *The Church of Frank Sinatra.*

---

2   *Birth of the Cool*—Miles Davis Nonet. One of the seminal albums of the 1950s.

What does this tell us? It says your dreams of making meaningful music do not depend on being several levels above where you can play. You can make the most profound music in terms of inner and outer results by turning on and tuning in! *Get off on the voice you have.* Thus, the power of the Inner Voice. The connection may be spiritual, it may be sensual, or comical, it may even be perverse. It doesn't matter. The only thing you can do is miss your inner voice's true motivation. If you're a sex addict, connect with your obsession when you sing. If you have a guru, connect with him or her. Connect with your power, not somebody else's. Don't be distracted with *the state of the art.* Be engulfed by your own *inner state.* The True You. Become addicted to your own need for inner expression. That is your power, your charisma.

So how shall I teach? I shall teach as I believe. What do I believe? That the fire of Miles Davis is the same fire that's in me. That the fire and genius of Miles Davis is also in you. We have to be willing to uncover it and surrender to it. I have such respect for the Miles Davises and Frank Sinatras of the world. They rode their own unique voices and the world followed. I was thinking that a nervous little kid from Long Island could not be a deep soul like these people. Perhaps I should be wearing a dashiki or skullcap. And of course, being Jewish, I was no stranger to a skullcap, but that would be the "wrong kind of skullcap." I found out that if I presumed there was a blazing light inside this kid from Long Island, as blazing as any other talent in the world, as deep as any philosopher and as passionate as any lover, I would find that strength and depth in me. It has taken me into my own zone of identification.

Note to singers

Singers, don't reach out when you sing, reach in. Reach into that joy, that sensuality. Reach in and let it bubble up and emerge as the sound of your voice, like Ella Fitzgerald, like the charisma of Frank Sinatra. Dig yourself hard the way Frank dug himself when he was singing. That's what the audience digs, *watching you dig yourself.* Let that joy bubble up and emerge, even as laughter, as it did with Ella Fitzgerald, when she was scatting on *The Lady Is a Tramp* The joy was just overwhelming. Singers, reach in, not out.

Parables 1

B.B. King, blues legend, in *Guitar Magazine:* "People ask me how I get my sound out of the guitar. I tell them that it is the same way you get the tone when you talk. It's just me. I could take your guitar, mine or anybody else's, and any amplifier, and get the same sound."

Parables 2

Once a merchant told a holy man who liked to preach, "You are really full of yourself, aren't you?" The holy man replied, "Of course I am. What are you full of?"

19 ■ The Maya of Music

Maya is the power in creation by which limitations and divisions seem to exist in the Oneness that is true reality. It is cosmic illusion, literally, "the measurer."

With great love and deference to those named Maya, in Sanskrit the word means "illusion." I thought "The Maya of Music" would make a good topic for a book, but I probably wouldn't have had a book's worth of stuff for it. It certainly can occupy a chapter. What are some of the thoughts about music that could be *maya?*

1   Music is important.

I once heard a musician announce to the audience, "Support the arts! Music isn't a luxury, it's a necessity!" I really thought about this. I wanted to put it to the test. Was it a necessity? Was it something I couldn't survive, *literally survive,* without? No, that would be my breathing, then food, water, and on from there. If there was no music, the world would be a drab, dour place. It would probably be a horrible world greatly lacking in spirit and even more steeped in violence, *but we could continue to exist.*

My spiritual teacher's path is filled with music. Music occupies a very important place in the journey of attaining The Self. That is a great place for me to be. I always assumed music was the nectar of truth. However, music is not necessarily a feature of every path, beautiful though it may be. Once I had the honor to play a fundraiser for the Dalai Lama. I met him and instantly felt I had a friend. He missed the music so he didn't hear me play; another pianist had the honor of playing on stage right in front of him. When he finished, someone asked His Holiness how he liked the pianist. The Dalai Lama said, "Well, I don't know music, but he looked happy while he was playing." I was shocked! Music was completely irrelevant to his message. I must admit I found it refreshing to see his happiness and compassion, and no music! So obviously, the truth is revealed in many ways.

The original premise of *Effortless Mastery* is that most of us play better when we don't consider our playing to be so important. With that understanding, not overemphasizing music's importance might just make it flow more freely.

2   What you're doing is important.

There is a more mundane state of mind, from where a great number of musicians operate, which finds music important, not because of its deep, intrinsic value, but because of what has grown monumentally important—*how well they play.*

Are they successful? The intrinsic value of art, which may or may not have been the prime motivation at the start, has decayed into a daily self-esteem check. *How do I sound? How do I sound now? How good am I today?*

I would say if you took 1 and 2 combined, if music becomes all about how well you play, the music itself becomes monumentally *unimportant*.

3   You are the creator of the music.

This has been discussed at length in other parts of the book. Of course, one may look at it this way and be highly successful. Or one may embrace the metaphysical model; he may consider himself to be the instrument. That understanding may take him to greater heights. Remember: *The power is faith!* I find I am much freer to go higher when I believe I am a cog in the wheel that brings the music to other souls, to animals, to vegetation, even to invisible vibrations on this planet, and other realms.

4   Music completes you.

You are already complete. *Music is not who you are, it's what you do.* What is your true value? That is a spiritual question to be answered, or not, by each one of us. *Who are you?* Again, if you value your life based on how you play and you buckle under pressure, doesn't that create a lot more pressure?

5   Playing music makes you automatically special.

That is a misunderstanding most non-musicians have about musicians. People think that musicians are special because they play music. I like to tell the story of the musician and the cabdriver.

Musician calls for a cab, gets in the car. The cabdriver says, "So what do you do?"

The musician says, "I'm a musician."

You always see that look in the cabdriver's eye in the rear-view mirror. He's thinking, *Wow! I have a musician in the car! He's so special, so creative. And here I am just driving a cab. I wish I had his life.*

Meanwhile the musician, self-obsessed, tormented by thoughts of doubt and inadequacy, looks at the cabdriver and thinks, *Wow, his life is so uncomplicated. Just get up each day and drive a cab. It would be so simple. I wouldn't have to make all these difficult decisions and think about my playing all the time.*

Music doesn't automatically make anyone free. Some think if they study Brazilian music, they'll be joyous, because Brazilian music is joyous. If they play reggae, they'll be liberated. Guess what? Brazilian music isn't necessarily joyous, *people are joyous!* If the music is played by a joyous person, then Brazilian music is joyous! They may find that from another state of mind, Brazilian music is not joyous, Reggae is not liberating.

Then there's "free music." A good joke is musicians trying to play free music *correctly!* Please hear this: ***The only free music is music that's free from self-judgment.*** In that sense, any music can be free!

Self-obsession is very common in all kinds of artists. Just being one hardly makes you special. Civilians assume that musicians aren't hobbled by the same neurotic, anal-retentive and small-minded stuff that they are. *NOT!* They can be just as small minded and neurotic, if not more so.

6   Your performance defines you.

The great player balances his achievements with humility, and the underperforming player needs to balance his disappointments with self-love. Nothing about performance should color the value of yourself. Too often we value ourselves by the level of our job, our performance, our salary, etc. It's hard not to do, but an essential thing to learn.

7   Music is hard or difficult.

In my first book, *Effortless Mastery* I said that it's better to regard music as *unfamiliar,* rather than "difficult." If you believe that music is difficult, you will learn it, even play it correctly, but *with difficulty.* That's what you would expect. But if you practice the affirmation "music is easy" over a lifetime, you begin to expect the pieces to become easy. It is a very different viewpoint to say, "Oh, this piece seems very difficult. I must not be *familiar* with it yet."

This is a great understanding. Before you adequately know a subject it always seems difficult. In music, each new key you play in seems harder than the last, but is it? Of course not. It's just less familiar than the one you've already become familiar with. Ease is a great measure of whether you've practiced something enough. Anything you play with ease never feels difficult. Therefore, it's better to replace the belief that **music is hard or difficult** with *music is easy. If it appears hard, I haven't become familiar with it yet.* Build that idea into your core belief system. It takes time and repetition.

8   If you beat yourself up enough, you can shame yourself into being a better musician.

Just the opposite. Why does playing inspire such fear? Every time you disappointed yourself, you didn't just play bad, you *felt bad about yourself*. The combination of two delusions is at play here. 1) You judge yourself as a person by how good a player you are, and, 2) You think you need to care more, try more, or guilt yourself more for not working hard enough, etc. The problem is that leads to a downward spiral. The more you care, the worse you feel and the worse you feel, the harder you try to play well, and the harder you try to play well . . . get it?

9   There are people in the world who were born to be deeper or more profound musicians than you.

I remember I used to think musicians coming from Brazil, Africa, or, for that matter, New York or Chicago, were deeper or more profound than I, who came from Long Island. We can fall into the trap of considering others more deserving of recognition, with deeper thoughts to express. We can assume they hail from a geographically or sociologically better place to be an artist, or that one ethnicity or another is more likely to be free and creative. This delusion is really important to dissolve.

Negative images of oneself can be the silent saboteur of all our efforts to succeed. I come from Long Island, New York. I felt such shame around that fact. People used to mock people from Long Island. They would pronounce it Looon Giland, which was sort of a Long Island accent.

I wrote about Long Island in *Effortless Mastery*. When another musician asked where I was from, I didn't say Long Island. I said, "New York." They could assume I was from the city. But when I saw people from other countries in dashikis, I thought they naturally had more wisdom than I did. Back in the day, a lot of white hipsters lamented they weren't Black. It was assumed that all black musicians not only had more rhythm, but had something more to say. Cultural conditions can make some of those assumptions true, but no one is blocked from the kingdom of heaven, so to speak. In my journey, as I started to scratch deeper and deeper beneath the surface, I lost my sense of identity as a little Jewish kid from Long Island. I have reached deep places within me because I assumed those depths existed. All people can become as deep and profound as they are willing to believe they are.

10 Music is the message.

That's one possible way of looking at it. But another way that may get more mileage is *music is the messenger*. In other words, if you believe there's something larger than music itself, it can extend the power of music to describe it. How much art and music has been dedicated to a higher purpose of some kind? How much more meaning has the music had?

11 Just playing great or being technically impressive is enough.

That may be true in a practical sense. You can make a career of showing an impressive technique. But it means you think you are valid because you have technical prowess, or invalid because you don't.

12 Consonance and dissonance, do they exist?

That is a complete invention of humans. You walk outside; you hear a car horn, a dog barking, street cleaner, four radios, etc. You don't say, "Wow, how dissonant the sounds are out here today!" In a certain state of mind, you might declare that *there is no dissonance!*

13 That any note you play is less significant than any other.

What belief would serve you better, that there are better and worse sounding notes or that *every note is the voice of God?* Both may be true, neither may be true. What is true is not important; *it's what you believe!* And, which belief would get you more mileage?

14 Why be inhibited when touching the piano when you don't even play piano?

People approach the piano with such trepidation, like it matters what keys they hit. Children use it. Adults lose it.

15 Over and over again: Don't value yourself as a person by how well you perform.

Being human is a gift of inestimable value. The Hindus believe that we go through thousands of lifetimes to finally attain a human birth. Don't contract the gift to such narrow proportions.

20  Fear Summary

For musicians but others can probably relate.

Fear of:

touching the instrument

not playing well

not being fulfilled

losing the beat

others playing better than you

hearing other good players

not succeeding

not swinging

people not noticing you

not being able to practice all the stuff you need

practicing the wrong stuff

not get a gig

getting a gig and messing it up

playing wrong notes!

letting go, because if you do you might mess up

others becoming successful

others sounding great

Bitterness over:

never becoming fluid in your playing

not being given enough talent

not being given a chance to play with the big boys

not swinging

others becoming successful

others playing better than you

even younger ones playing better than you!

Having a family instead of moving to New York

still messing up the bridge to *All the Things You Are*

life passing you by

who the media and the record companies like and don't like

no jazz club in your area

your solos not being not important

you not being important

your playing determining your self-worth

having to be able to play every kind of jazz

others being real players and not you

others being real people and not you

others having it and you don't

etc. . . . etc. . . .

Because of fear (ego) you:

try too hard to play

lose the beat

try to be something you're not

try to love music you don't

rush, stumble

practice a million things without absorbing anything

don't go to hear other musicians play (they might be too good!)

are jealous of other's gifts and talents

are jealous of other's opportunities and good fortunes

don't practice at all

don't swing

can't focus

put yourself down a lot

prop yourself up a lot

don't meet people eye-to-eye

stop loving

To rid yourself of this gunk, you must transcend the mind and enter the heart. There you will learn to:

love yourself

breathe deeply

see your self-worth in spiritual terms

learn inner peace and joy that isn't dependent on your playing

find the "inner space," and reside there

play from the inner space

practice from the inner space

love others unconditionally

love yourself unconditionally

practice methodically and patiently, knowing your quest is attaining mastery and not simply "needing to get better"

play freely and creatively, loving every note you play

be content with whatever cards you've been dealt

wish other musicians well (ouch!)

derive joy from your life and your music

express that light through effortless playing

Why can't you let go?

1. You can't give yourself permission to let, go because you're not willing to play poorly and still love yourself.

2. You haven't mastered the basic elements of music (time changes, rhythm, form, etc.), so if you let go, you'll mess it all up.

21 ■ Meditation #3

There has been a lot of discussion thus far about *The Space* and the intellect, between the Self and the self-conscious, and so on. What lives on the inside, beneath our awareness? How do we get distracted and diverted from our own powerful Selves?

Now we explore the way to stay conscious on the inside while perceiving outer realms—how to stay inwardly connected while outwardly engaged.

Take a comfortable position.

Close your eyes. Now follow your breath. Notice your breath. I know you're breathing or you wouldn't be reading this book or following this meditation. Don't exaggerate your breath but just notice that you are breathing. Don't let it become "special." You might notice the slight increase in tension as the lungs expand when you inhale. You might notice a slight release when you exhale. But don't make much out of it. Just observe it. Now that I've described it, do that for five breaths. Notice you are breathing for five breaths . . .

OK, now open your eyes. With eyes open, keep focusing on your breath. Instead of getting involved in what you're looking at, instead of responding to the stimuli, stay inside and continue to notice that you are breathing . . .

Now take a break. Shake your body out a bit. If you want to think, think, scratch an itch, whatever. Take one minute to do that . . .

Now become still again and close your eyes . . . Again, tune inside your body and simply notice you are breathing. No expansion from here, we're not leading to anything great. Nope, this is it. Just close your eyes and notice you're breathing . . .

Now open your eyes but continue to pay attention *inside* to the fact that you are breathing. Perhaps spend two minutes with eyes open but inwardly focused on your breathing.

Now take a break. Walk around the room. If it's a small room, go out to another room or go outside and walk, perhaps in a circle three times. If it's a child have him run round in a circle as many times as he can in two minutes.

Now come back to where you were. Get comfortable and close your eyes. Now count five breaths. As you do, notice everything you can about those breaths. How they go in, how they go out. Then open your eyes. And with eyes open, count five more . . .

Now you're done. Before you move on, close your eyes again for a minute and hear this suggestion:

What you've done is the easiest way to drop right into *The Space*. Don't you feel a little different? Didn't you feel different the first time we did it? We closed our eyes and followed our breath. Don't call it meditation. When I do that, my next thought is, "Oh, I don't do that very well." But anyone can notice they're breathing, or count their breaths as easily as they can count cars on the highway.

I'll give you a little assignment if you want to try it. As you move through your day, stop a few times whenever it occurs to you, close your eyes for a moment, and notice the next three breaths. Then open your eyes and continue to notice three more breaths. This is a quick and dependable way to get a small sampling, a whiff, so to speak, of living and experiencing your life from *The Space*. If it ends quickly, don't mourn it's passing. Don't expect it to stay, and don't expect any change in your behavior, or in your day. No change, no big deal, just an easy exercise you can do whenever you think of it. Don't look for progress. Let the results unfold, if there are any.

Stand up, stretch, come out of it and go on to your next activity. Just imagine greeting every moment of your day from this inner connection. (*What a day this has been, what a rare mood I'm in. Why its . . . Almost Like Being in Love!*)[1]

---

1 "Almost Like Being in Love"—a popular American song from 1947, written by Frederick Lowe and Alan Jay Lerner

22 ■ Comparison of Eastern and Western Thought and Music

My general impressions are of East and West, in terms of philosophy and spirituality, are as follows: In the West, we always think we are inventing the wheel. In the East, they know the wheel already exists and is perfect. So, progress for a follower of Eastern spirituality is learning to *tune into and rely on the perfection that already exists.* (OK. That's it for generalities about West and East!)

Music history gives us examples. In the West, we followed a path, the pre-existence of which we were unaware. Western music "discovered" new intervals that evolved into what we call Western classical music. The order in which we discovered those intervals almost identically follows the harmonic series,[1] which has always existed.

---

1 Harmonic Series: A set of frequencies consisting of a fundamental and the harmonics related to it by an exact fraction, the harmonic partials of a single tone. For example, when you hear the fundamental tone, what you don't hear is the harmonic series that happens at the same time. The octave, fifth, fourth, third and so on. All that is the nature of a single pitch.

The Eastern musician presumes that all the harmony in the universe is apparent. What they strive for is to attune their ear and their awareness to this reality. If they attain a state of receptivity, *Harmony reveals* itself. (Again, note the capitalization of the word *Harmony*: the *Infinite*, the *Supreme Power*. Then recall the title of the book, *Becoming The Instrument*.)

That's why the concept of *raga*[2] in Indian music has never and will never change. There is a way that the succession of notes in raga interacts with the harmonics that exist above the auditory capabilities of the ear—beyond the physical. They also accept that since this entire world, the entire universe, is made of Vibration (capitalizing for the same reason because *Vibration is God*), how they interact with those vibrations, harmonics, overtones, etc., actually affects all levels of reality, from the physical universe—matter—to other layers of consciousness, even to the behavior of Living Beings and all of Nature. (Ditto.)

They have morning ragas, evening ragas, ragas that bring light, and others that bring rain. There are ragas that evoke devotion, love, tenderness, nobility, and so forth. In other words, *ragas evoke virtues*. The Indian musician is as interested in developing those virtues as in mastering technique. For this reason. *Raga never changes.*

Just classifying this as East and West is overly simplistic, I realize. There are more ways to look at the world than East—West. Some of the "Eastern" ways of looking at life are found in other cultures. The Middle East has long been a cradle of mysticism—from the Gnostics to the Sufis. You find the same musical goals and philosophies in the mys-

2   Raga: A raga, or raag, is a melodic framework for improvisation akin to a melodic mode in Indian classical music.

tical traditions of Judaism. One might break it down to industrial versus ancient folk cultures, even rich versus poor. For example, the continent of Africa is categorized into East, West, North and South. Yet, the musical philosophy, spirituality, and universal connection of the indigenous peoples throughout the continent are very "Eastern."[3] African musicians aim to express life, in all its aspects, through the medium of sound. Then there are the worshipers of Santeria, utilizing the Bata drum, which is Cuban and Puerto Rican (Also owing very much to Africa). The purpose, unlike "the West," is not to innovate so much as to celebrate. It all roughly translates to the following:

> Everything is comprised of vibration. A fact of life for sages throughout millennia is now confirmed by science. Quantum physics is where science and spirituality start to integrate. As scientists make newer and newer "discoveries," they are arriving on the doorstep of mystics, shamans, monks, sages and the like who have understood reality through enlightened perception, or reception. I'll roughly define "Western thought" as trying to understand the universe through the conscious mind or "science," rather than receiving its mysteries through Universal Mind. (Oops. God again!)

I must allude here to a drug experience to illustrate how the expansion of mind, by any means, aids us in hearing and seeing connections that were previously hidden. One night back in those good old '70s, I had taken some acid in my apartment. The mystical event I submitted myself to with awe and respect was called *evening*. Anyway, this night I listened to three different types of music: Indian classical

---

3   We must apply these observations to indigenous peoples only, for in all cases their conquerors were European, hence, "Western philosophy and religion."

music, the source of which I don't remember (where are all those cassette tapes?); Joni Mitchell's album, *Court and Spark;* and finally, to the Bela Bartok string quartets.

That night, in my expanded awareness, I heard vibrations, overtones, and harmonics interacting on levels I had never heard before, but they were all interrelated. The difference was the frequency, not of pitch but of *vibratory activity*. Joni's were at one cycle, Bartok's were at a faster cycle, and finally, shifting into high gear were the frequencies of the ragas. *They were all related.*

Now this doesn't particularly sound like the farthest out acid story, though I do have some of those, but the vibratory relationships I detected while on the drug were real because I heard them many times after that. Of course, the validity could be challenged, because one hour later I jumped out of my second-floor window and broke both legs. (Only kidding! Someday I'll reveal the *other* acid trip stories!)

A story

One of our earliest examples of Western music is Gregorian chant.[4] This was music of the church sung in unison. To harmonize with it might have been cause to be burned at the stake! Here was the brotherhood, singing away, everyone on the same pitch, when one day a boy came in and asked the director in a high voice, "Hey mister director, could I please sing with you guys?"

The director invited him to sit in and everything he sang was an octave higher than the rest of the monks. The director freaked out! He said, "Are you kidding me, get the

4   Gregorian Chant: Church music sung as a single vocal line in free rhythm and a restricted scale (plainsong), in a style developed for the medieval Latin liturgy.

hell out of here. We can't tolerate this unbearable dissonant squealing you're doing. Leave!"

Quietly, the priest came up to the director and confided to him, "You know, Sol, this kid is the nephew of one of our biggest benefactors. He told me he'd really appreciate it if you could include him in the choir, and he'll be glad to show his appreciation."

The director nodded, sighed, and said, "OK young man, you can sing with us." They endured his squealing until it didn't feel so alien anymore. Some radicals actually started to like it and wrote it into the music, and the *octave*[5] was born!

They prattled on for seventy-five years or so. One day, a farmer came into the church and said to the director, "Uh, mister, I hate to bother you, you seem to be busy rehearsing and all that, but I just entered the priesthood and they told me if I became a priest, I could sing with y'all."

The director at that time looked at him sternly and inquired with squinting eyes, "Well, can you sing?"

The farmer's face lit up and he said, "Can I sing? Boy, can I! You just put me in there coach and watch, eh, I mean, listen to me!"

The director snorted, "Very well, stand over there."

As they started to sing, the director immediately noticed that the man had a tin ear. Every note the monks sang, this man sang a *fifth*[6] away! Exactly the fifth! He was nowhere near the same pitch as either the high singers or the low singers, but right in the middle. The director yelled, "*YOU*— you nincompoop! Get out of my choir right now and get lost!"

---

5   The Octave: The same note 12 "semitones" higher or lower.
6   The Fifth: An interval of two notes 7 semitones apart

The farmer was crushed and slowly started to leave when one of the board members of the church came up quietly behind the director and whispered, "Ah . . . Herr Director, we have a situation here. This farmer is wealthy and has a family. We convinced him to renounce all his worldly possessions and become a monk. Now instead of leaving his worldly goods to his family, he has assigned them all to the church. We'd *really* appreciate it if you could relax your standards . . . *just a bit* . . . and allow this fine brother to sing with the choir."

The director looked skyward, palms upturned, sighed and cried, *"Why hast thou forsaken me?"* But, after all, the director had a family to support and this was good paying job. Dutifully he turned to the farmer, pointed to a spot in the choir and said, "Please, take your place," and in only fifty short years, the musicians had endured, and *the fifth* was an acceptable "modern harmony." They sang in fifths.

Then there's the story fifty years later of the gardener who blackmailed the director and forced him to let him sing in the choir because he had seen him romping with the bishop's maid, and he couldn't even sing in tune with the guy who sang a fifth away from the melody, and the fourth[7] was born. And so on . . . Of course, I jest. "Innovation" in Western music was the movement from unison, to octaves, to fifths and fourths. In Medieval music, you hear harmonies of fifths and fourths. Examples are readily available in Technicolor B-movies about kingdoms, knights, Moses and such made during the 1950s. (Some of us learned *everything* from American kitsch!) Eventually Western classical music

---

7   The Fourth: A note 5 semitones above or below another note

evolved to the intervals of major and minor thirds[8] and—
voila!—the true classical era was ushered in.

Ah, the major and minor third! The heartache, the triumph, all the dramas of the human condition are described
by the use of major or minor. You'll never hear a soundtrack
for a documentary about the Holocaust played in a major
key. Today, major and minor are still the dominant (no pun
intended)[9] music of our culture.

Moving forward again into supposedly unexplored territory was the minor second.[10] This enabled the liberal use the
chromatic scale.[11] This one innovation accounts for the entire
Romantic period in music. Chopin, Liszt, and composers like
these, wrote dripping, romantic melodies, and chromatic
harmonies for accompaniment. You can hear these themes
in movies about these composers—again the Technicolor
B-movies of the 1940s, '50s and '60s, or any movie that
Liberace[12] starred in. (I suppose you could just listen to the
music of Chopin and Liszt. *Never thought of that!)*

By the 20th century, composers were investigating what is
called twelve-tone music.[13] This is a "system" that combined
intervals and "rows" of notes that don't have to obey the harmonies of all the previous incarnations of classical music.
The clash and cluster that could be experienced in some
"20th century music" is where the public decided, *"we've had*

8   Major and Minor Third: The major is 4 semitones up or down from a note, the
    minor is 3.
9   A musician's joke!
10 Minor Second: The smallest interval, 1 semitone from another note
11 Chromatic Scale: Every semitone from a note back to the same note an octave
    higher or lower
12 Liberace: A schlocky, schmaltzy, kitschy pop classical pianist popular in
    America from the 1950s through much of the rest of the century.
13 Twelve-Tone Music: Related to, or being *serial* music utilizing the twelve
    chromatic tones. The music is considered very dissonant to the novice listener

enough!" (I am avoiding the elephant in the room, the virtue of all of these musics and the virtue of *listening* to them.)

So, while the Western musician was changing and evolving, the Eastern musician was attuning himself to the harmony that already existed in the universe.

John Cage[14] composed *Four Minutes And 33 Seconds of Silence.* Composed it! It was an idea more than a piece of music, but Cage had the right idea at the right time. So, in the West, Cage invents "Silence." Of course, silence existed long before that composition, like at the beginning of everything. Mystics of many traditions acknowledge *The Primordial Silence: Brahma*, the *Absolute.* It is understood as many things but one definition I like is, "vastness of Pure Mind." All music arises and subsides like waves in the ocean. Silence is the ocean itself.

It may sound like I'm making a value judgment. I'm not. There are strong cases to be made for both East and West. The excitement of the entire history of Western music would be null in void if we had all gone east. And without the wisdom of the East, we might have blown ourselves up by now. No, God, *IHE*,[15] (please check note below) gave us both faculties from which to describe His creation, and we have neither the width, breadth nor depth to decide what faculty should be predominant.

I think I will just add here that one could make the argument that from the point of view of just intervals, Western classical music stopped evolving harmonically at the turn of the 20th century. We stopped moving to smaller intervals at

14   John Cage (September 5, 1912—August 12, 1992) was an American composer, music theorist, artist, and philosopher. One of the leading figures of the post-war avant-garde.

15   Perhaps we can invent a new initial, like BCE. or CE. to meet this situation. After the word "God" would be IHE. *If He Exists.* Your thoughts?

the shores of the well-tempered scale,[16] semi-tones being the smallest interval.

Many amazing developments have happened in Western music in the 20th century, jazz being the most spectacular of them all. Jazz musicians were using the same twelve tones in different combinations to express different passions. Jazz has provided endless ways to rediscover the twelve tones and innovate within the vast element of rhythm.[17] But in a sense, when Arnold Schoenberg[18] introduced twelve-tone music, we could say that from the point of view of intervals, Western classical music hasn't progressed since about 1901! But this is an argument for another book. (Not a very important one either!)

For a great part of the 20th century, there have been musicians actively engaged in *microtonal music,*[19] which would be the only way to go further, (or smaller), but the practitioners are a small minority. The stumbling block for most musicians who want to foray further into harmonic "innovation" is the reality that most conventional instruments feature only the twelve notes. One would have to relearn everything. Octaves of twenty-four, thirty-six, or any number of notes could be

16 The Well-Tempered Scale: in musical tuning, a temperament is a tuning system that slightly compromises the pure intervals of just intonation to meet other requirements.

17 One might surmise that it was conditions beyond music itself that led to the creation of jazz: oppression, slavery, heartache, forcible removal of an entire group of people from their homeland, and persistent discrimination after the fact. These unfortunate events do confirm, however, that *music is always stronger when it's motivated by something larger than itself.*

18 Arnold Schoenberg (September 1874–13 July 1951) was an Austrian-American composer who created new methods of musical composition involving atonality, namely serialism and the 12-tone row.

19 Microtonal intervals are intervals of less than a semitone

created, or one could can create their own scales through endless tunings. A few courageous and ambitious musicians have made careers out of this, but precious few.[20]

I was once asked way back in the 20th century, "What will the evolution of music be in the 21st century?"

I answered, "I think the important question is what the evolution of the *musician* will be." Artists from every path are increasingly curious about who they are, what makes art important and how to blend their talents and ideas to express something beyond their limited selves. Eastern musicians are collaborating with Western musicians to create new and wondrous fusions. The musicians of India, Africa, the Middle East, and other parts of Asia are as fascinated with us as we are with them. Perhaps there's the possibility of *becoming one light!* On some level, we are all surrendering the confines of our conscious minds compared to the limitless landscape of the Universal Mind. Perhaps our salvation lies in this quest, if it can be accomplished. No one knows how much pain we will need to endure before we surrender to The Grand Reality en masse.

Religion and spirituality

For me "God's Grace" is analogous to the sun. The sun never withholds itself and is always available if we are just willing to stand in our driveways and turn our faces towards it. It's always ready to shed its light on us. The sun doesn't care if we avail ourselves of its light or not, yet it is always available, *without judgment.* I think it's pretty universal in all re-

20   It should be further pointed out that various microtonal systems have always been prevalent in ancient ethnic music around the world. Not everyone was persuaded by the *well-tempered scale!*

ligions that God is love. Yet how can we be one with He/ She/It/They if we don't love ourselves? (Hmm . . . If I called it She/He/It/They . . . I could cover the gender of God with the initials *S H I T !* Naw, even I don't have *balls that big . . .*)

It is very dangerous to paint all religious groups with the same brush, e.g., confusing the Muslim faith with those who would kill in the name of Islam. If you look at the words of Jesus, the Baal Shem Tov, Muhammed, St. Thomas, St. Francis, the Sufi Poet Rumi, Vietnamese Buddhist Monk Thich Nhat Hanh, the Dalai Lama, the words of the Kabbalah, or writings of early Christian Mysticism, they are all strikingly similar. That's why I prefer a spiritual path to a religion. A spiritual path shines light on wisdom regardless of its source. Some religions may confine themselves to the "authorities" of their particular religion. Jesus spoke of love, peace, mercy and compassion, yet it wasn't long before people killed each other in his name.

The same thing happens in music. Charlie Parker played language of a new freedom—Bebop. Only a few years later, the term imprisoned others who wished to express themselves differently. Even free music became dogma. I was told that while John Coltrane was playing his free music there were "judges" on the sidelines proclaiming that it *wasn't free enough.* Fortunately, the Inquisition didn't follow. (After all, *it is only music!)*

Once someone asked me, "Don't you have to be talented to be a musician?" He is a person who is steeped in Eastern spirituality and lives his whole life in service of its concepts.

I asked him, "Is there anyone who cannot be God?"

Knowing that the basis of his understanding is that everyone *is God* he smiled and said "No."

I asked, "Then how can someone *not* be a musician?" (By now you must be thinking that you're reading a book from the most spiritual agnostic you've ever heard . . . could be . . .)

I think the spiritual heart of every religion says the same thing. But the language of different time periods, different priorities, and different countries have affected the wording. Also affecting it was the way future generations would hear the message and more importantly, *through what ear would they listen?* Would they hear it from their small self, the ego, or would they receive the message by attuning to Universal Mind? If you look back on history through this lens, you can see how every variation of belief evolved in relation to the conditions on the ground, so to speak. Would the message be heard the same way by warriors, artists, merchants or politicians?

In so-called modern times, say, the mid-20th century on, the West has been positively influenced by the East. The power of song and chant has emerged as a healing force in many religious groups. Meditation has become a critically important practice in many circles: religious, medical and scientific. Drum circles in the tradition of Africa are popular.

Religious boundaries pit us against one other. It's a simple fact that millions of people have been slaughtered in the name of one religion or another. I think the real test is to focus on the spiritual heart of the path and embody it. If we do, we're much more likely to respect other paths. I've *come to believe* that God gave the world addiction *to cure us of religious zealotry.* The spirit and intent of *The Twelve Steps* is in remarkable harmony with Buddhism. Nothing like an addiction to humble fanatics.

I have a dream

As it was once famously said, *"I have a dream."* In my dream, all the people of the earth are looking skyward with excitement and expectation. Each thinks his prophet is coming or that the time will come when God Himself will appear and put things right. One group says God is this, another says God is that. Still another says they're both wrong. Five different sects follow the same messiah and say each other is wrong! Still another group insists *he doesn't even exist.* One sect believes they have the "evidence." Many believe that those who don't join their sect are going to hell. But in my dream on this day, their faces are all turned skyward, because there is a great rumbling. Something is about to happen! Suddenly, out from these rolling clouds emerges God, kind of like the alien mother ship in the movie *Independence Day* (Not *Independence Day II!*).

Different religious leaders point to the sky excitedly and say, "See, I told you, God is this!" But others point and say, "You're crazy, now you can see, God has always been that!" Still others have completely different versions of what they're seeing and they all correspond perfectly to *what their beliefs are at the time.* Perhaps man does create God in his own image after all, or in the image *of his faith.*

Just then, all their divergent visions become one. A great light fills the sky, the light of a thousand suns, and the heat, too. At first there are cries of torment, the light and heat are so great that it's burning away everyone's clothes, skin, flesh, bone, tendons, intestines, and, finally, *their minds,* until everything has been consumed by the *Great Light.* All that remains where each one was standing is a *Column of Light.* Now all those people around the world are columns of light.

They all look the same, like billions of light sabers all over the globe. After a minute or two, all the lights start merging into one great light, which then merges with the great light in the sky and . . . we are all *One Great Light*. We are home.

I want to relate a story that I think illustrates the One Great Truth beneath the myriad of separations.

For a time, I was blessed to play with a great Jewish clarinet player, Andy Statman. Andy is a transcendent musician *because of his inner state*. I felt Andy Statman was to Jewish music what John Coltrane was to so-called Afro/jazz, using modes of Hebrew music[21] with spiritual motivation, combined with jazz and improvisation.

Being in Andy's world a bit allowed me to see a side of the Jewish faith that I hadn't experienced. Growing up in Long Island, I didn't see a lot of spirituality in Judaism. I think it depends on what temple you went to (and *"Who's your Rabbi?"*).[22] Now I was able to hang out in Brooklyn with the Hassidim and got a closer look than ever before. I met many amazing people there. Evidently, there are a number of sects of Hassidim, and this was a more mystical one: Breslov. It reminded me of the yogic path I follow. They were sweet people with amazing faith and discipline. It was so good for me to see the mystical heart of Judaism. I think they would have liked to bring me back into the fold, but my heart had already been claimed by another guru.

But even here there were customs that I could not abide. I believe that because of that time in history when humanity was much more tribal, all the beautiful wisdom expressed

---

21   The Well-Tempered Scale: in musical tuning, a temperament is a tuning system that slightly compromises the pure intervals of just intonation to meet other requirements.

22   "Who's Your Daddy?"

seemed to be for "the Jewish people." Andy's manager is Hasidic scholar Rabbi Dovid Sears, who has written books about the Baal Shem Tov, the creator of Hasidic Judaism, and his grandson known as Rebbe Nachman of Breslov, who in his time was the leader of the Breslov sect.

One night, Dovid and I were talking on the phone. He was telling me the spoken wisdom of the Hassidim. I was telling him the wisdom of the gurus I follow. Their thoughts were almost identical. It really showed us that behind all the divisions there really is one Universal truth, or set of truths. At one point, he recited one of these beautiful thoughts but at the end of the quote were the words, "of the Jewish people." I had to tell him that that's where we parted ways. What he had just said was absolute truth, but how could it only apply to one group of people? Could God be that provincial?

I pointed out to him that the difference between a spiritual path and a religion is that the spiritual path will illuminate wisdom from any path so that its followers cannot fail to see, and be reminded of, The Truth. To give him an example, I had a stack of maybe fifty magazines, a publication of the path I follow where different devotees contribute articles, along with writings from the guru and quotes from spiritual teachers of every culture, every religion.[23] I randomly pulled one of the magazines out and before I could open it, I noticed a quote on the back page. I said, "Guess what Dovid? I just reached for any book, any quote, and without even opening one of them, I saw a quote on the back page. Guess who it is? The Baal Shem Tov!"

After a dramatic pause, David whispered, "Mind Blowing!" *That's the Shakti for you!*

Finally, what I most love about specifically Indian philosophy is its emphasis on words like *intoxication, bliss, nectar, compassion, joy, blessings, God's creativity, God's play*. Intoxication, ah—music to an addict's ears! For it is the true intoxication, the intoxication of the *Supreme Self,* and the true addiction to *bliss*, that beguiles me and fills me with longing. *And that's is why I play!*

Western musicians may be on the precipice of becoming spiritual instruments, contemplating the meaning of *why they play*. Musicians of India have always known this and it is part of their training. Their teachers are referred to as "gurus."

Fear of God and imposed morality, that's a turnoff. Regretfully, *it causes people to seek to control others.* Coincidently, *greed* seems to be a common ulterior motive, as can be seen throughout history.

There is another word in Indian religion. *Dharma. Dharma* is a Sanskrit word that means "the eternal and inherent nature of reality, regarded in Hinduism as a cosmic law underlying right behavior and social order." When one is in harmony with *Cosmic Law, Dharma* flows naturally. We don't impose it; we *surrender* to it. Again, it points to the idea that if we get into the proper alignment, the right results will flow. The music works *even when it doesn't. Right action flows naturally from the Inner Connection,* God *IHE,* if you will. *Moksha* is a word found in the scriptures of Hinduism, Jainism and Buddhism—all paths that originated in India. It means *liberation*.

That's what I seek as a musician and as a person. It's what I love about jazz. Jazz evolves thanks to the desire of the modern musician to transcend the constraints of the previous musicians. With respect, it seeks to break the dogma of the previous style and language. There are certain truths that transcend any dogmas, any structure that man invents, even if that structure's original intent was to preserve The Truth. There is One Great Power, One Great Light, and all else is imposing limited intellect on the Limitless One. I'll go with the idea that we are pure light, and our only sin is that *we don't know it*. How will this discourse help you be a better musician, a better researcher, soldier, technician, or laborer? Imagine being the total embodiment of this light, then *become the instrument*.

23 ■ Lessons from Music to Life

Lessons for all walks of life

1 Perfection already exists. It's humans who mess it up.

In music, I look at all the details: who the musicians are, how they are or aren't meshing, the tuning and quality of the piano, all of these things—without a lot of concern. I feel my problems dissolve as I approach the performance. The cacophony of what's working and what's not becomes a kind of perfection unto itself. I'm not centered in thoughts of what needs to happen. Accepting things as they are, even enjoying the chaos, is another kind of music. One who views the situation with equanimity can still focus. Faith and creativity thrive amongst the chaos. Ironically, wonderfully, they often get the best results.

2 Mistakes: Celebrate them! Don't be a hostage to success or failure!

Once, I was supposed to show up for jury duty. I'd been trying to arrange it for a convenient time. I had the perfect day lined up, but I forgot to call the night before to see if I was due to come in. Had I called the night before and shown up, I would have been let go immediately, and that would have been that. My commitment would have been fulfilled for another four years. But I didn't call the night before, so when I showed up for jury duty, I wasn't allowed to check in. It was a double screw-up, because not only did I have to be reassigned to another day, but on the original day I had been assigned, everyone was dismissed!

I was having a great morning when this *mistake* happened. It was like pulling the plug on all the good energy and watching it go down the drain. Sound familiar? As I drove home from the courthouse, I kept reminding myself how I'd messed up, how great it would have been to have gotten my responsibility out of the way, but I'd blown it.

Then I tried to observe what I was going through and remain as they say, *mindful.* As I became more of a witness to my consciousness, I could feel my body chemistry change. The sense of optimism I'd felt that morning morphed into a state of discontent and self-recrimination. I thought about how different it would have been had it been a mistake in music.

There I possess a natural detachment. It is my experience that when I welcome mistakes, I make a lot fewer of them. When they happen, so what? The person who becomes the instrument makes many fewer mistakes if he knows that *mistakes are part of perfection!*

If we can view our mistakes *in life* the same way, we can feel the full throttle of our power, compassion, self-love, love of others, and flow of ideas. Embrace the darkness and return to the light with greater ease.

3 Practice contentment with what is. Receive whatever comes with gratitude, not expectation.

Regard all your output and success to be a gift, which doesn't increase arrogance, but gratitude. The more we desire, the harder it is to harmonize ourselves with what actually is. In this sense, **the more we ask for, the less we receive.** Religions, spiritual paths, psychological and psychiatric principles, neuroscience, all these paths allude to a space within one's own being that is undisturbed by factors on the ground, because it is always in tune with everything. That space inside is naturally attuned to this moment—reality as it is, not as we would wish it to be. It doesn't mean you don't "go for it." It means you apply all your talents, ingenuity, cleverness, and creativity and then *turn the results over to your Higher Power.* That is harmonizing one's self with life.

Take it from a thought junkie: the world of thoughts rarely provides comfort. It takes personal effort to learn the art of *receiving.*

4 No matter what work you do, drop your hands and take a breath.

Drop the hands from the piano, the computer, pen and paper, put down the saxophone, carpentry tools, whatever.

This can be one of the simplest and most profound innovations in your life. Feel when tension or angst arises and recognize that the quality of your work is about to diminish. *Learn to cherish the state of mind from which you are working more than the work itself requires.* You can't lose. It always produces a higher quality of work. I don't even rate my performances anymore by how well I play, but by how much I surrender. I've had much proof of the superior results, by any criteria.

5 Studying smaller amounts promotes a greater chance of ownership.

I've covered the psychological and even emotional reasons why we lose focus or become overwhelmed. Often, we are studying too much material. It's hard to say what the proper amount is for you. Let your own inner tension be your guide. Don't torment yourself with the "I should's." Honor the amount of concentration you have. That's part of honoring yourself. Don't expect your capacity to match someone else's.

Things in your job may be more difficult because of knowledge studied but not mastered. Moving forward with less than a full foundation of skills makes one seem dull witted or not very talented. Remember, mastery of small details beats an overview of many. Mastery isn't the end game; it's the opening bell. *It takes what it takes.* There's no other way.

The fundamentals of any subject are analogous to the installation of software. If the software is not properly installed, nothing functions as it should. For us, the "bug" in our software is our lack of preparation or insufficient knowledge. **It takes a lot of effort to be effortless.** Knowledge expressed in real time is absolutely necessary. On my Mac, when that color wheel is spinning and spinning, it is because some information in my computer is not immediately connecting with its intended destination, causing the *groove,* so to speak, to be interrupted.

In music, when the fundamentals are not fully installed, everything on the grid is greatly hampered. While music moves in tempo, or *real time,* lack of ownership causes a glitch, manifests out as plain old bad playing. The player cannot catch up. Therefore, mastering a smaller amount of information, rather than skimming large swaths, sets a tone of ownership. That builds a better engineer, musician, athlete, *a better instrument.*

Remember the example involving water: You have a certain amount of concentration. If your concentration is water, how deep it goes depends on the size of the container. The container is time and amount of information. Manage both so *the water runs deep.* In music, mastery of a few bars absolutely raises *the bar!* When you create deep understanding, it has a collateral effect. Everything gets easier. It also creates the standard by which you will expect to learn the next parcel of information. Absolute understanding trumps general understanding.

6 Allow *The Space* to tell you how much study you can handle.

Water = concentration. *The Space* = absolute clarity, a clear lake with no ripples, *in a state of absolute receptivity.* Receptivity = higher intelligence for solving problems beyond one's normal capabilities. Ideas arrive to "meet the need."

If we remember simply to drop our hands and take a breath when we lose *The Space, this single idea would be a revolutionary way to study!* Rejuvenate, follow your breathing and become empty again so you can work or play on the highest level. With renewed concentration and receptivity, focus on the next small area. We may have four hours, and our desire is to spend it working on our craft. But who's to say that four hours wouldn't be better as twenty-minute segments with breaks? Be sensitive to your capacity, honor it, work within it.

7 Practice loving yourself without evidence, unconditionally.

Don't wait until you're the right kind of person, have the right kind of job, etc. to love and honor yourself. That must be practiced for *its own sake.* Don't wait until you're noticed. *Practice noticing yourself.*

8 Look for brilliance from your team. Encourage it.

In my early days, when I first formed bands, I looked for people whose playing I liked, but I had too clear an idea of how I wanted them to play. They were talented musicians, but the more I told them, the more they played like, "What does the leader want me to do?" I have since learned to not only hire the most creative musicians, but to let them guide me to places *I hadn't thought of.* In one scenario, the flowers are dying the more you water them, and in the other you allow rain and sunlight to *do its thing.*

9   Speak what is true, not what sounds good.

Paradoxically, that is what draws people to you. When the little ego is at bay *it actually gets what it wants—respect!*

10   Be open to your true calling.

At Berklee, I am helping the students find their true voice and get to know what that feels like. Even if identifying their voice leads to changing careers, it helps them be attentive to where their true inspiration lies. All the wisdom and power one might need for their ultimate success can be learned in lessons found in the study of music. That's the lens though which we're looking at life in *Becoming The Instrument.* Many who study music, even many who've gone as far as graduating from college, may not become professional musicians. They may achieve success in other careers. This is a statistical fact. So, is it better to prepare exclusively for recitals and performances, or should the deeper lessons of practice and performance allow the student to gain wisdom that may lead to another, more successful career? The musical path may lead to finding one's true calling.

Many years ago, I had a student who was a professional musician and a good guitarist. He read in my first book something about not sticking with music as your primary function if your true passion lay elsewhere. He took it to heart and in the process, created an important innovation in the music world. He created ArtistShare. Years before GoFundMe, Brian Camelio invented the artist-fan model and changed the world.

I'll let him tell his story from there:

"I was really stuck on the idea of being a guitarist. I was so single minded. I based my identity on being a professional guitarist. But after studying with Kenny and reading his book, I realized I was in love with the *idea* of being a guitar player, not the actual process. It took a long time, but slowly I started steering towards things I loved. I found my great love was writing software.

"There were lots of parallels between composing and writing computer language. My creative mind drew parallels to what I learned from Kenny about composing, getting into *The Space,* working a motif from a detached mind, etc. But now I was doing something that actually *pleased me.* And because of that, I was very good at it. From there, I made a commitment to only doing things that I was absolutely passionate about. It took me a while. I was used to caring so much what other people thought. Or what *I thought they thought* about me. It was too much baggage, but my love of music was still there.

"It is in that spirit that I created ArtistShare. All my creativity was still going to celebrate the music process, but now I was enabling other artists to develop their own passion and create relationships with people through the software I was writing. It was so engaging and so much fun. The years have just flown by! Fast forward to a few years ago. I started to pick up music again, but not with the idea of expectation that anything was going to come out of it. I sit down and thoroughly enjoy myself. I do 45 minutes or so and then I'm done! Satisfied. And I can actually listen to music now without that little voice in my head saying, 'I'm better than that guy. Worse than that one, etc.' I never enjoyed listening so much.

"What I actually wanted from music was a feeling of connection. I was able to connect with other people and watch their connections happen because of what I had created. No ego trip, it just made me happy."

Brian became successful because he went into an area where he applied all the lessons of music to his true passion. When practicing guitar, he was so aware of the giants that had gone before him that it was hard for him to feel original or even authentic. In writing software, he had no one towering over him. He became *an artist*.

"Ideas didn't come from my brain; they came from my heart. *(The Space.)* Now I know whether I'm forcing an idea or if the idea is just coming through. Ninety percent of the ideas of ArtistShare came through me. I made it a point to always trust my gut." Brian has become the instrument. *What a relief!*

He's recently found a new idea that will innovate the industry again. "I've retooled the old model into label/ partner services." His model allows anyone to have their own record company and control their own destiny. "It's like a turnkey system: distribution, fulfillment, fan engagement, crowd funding, analytics, music-publishing administration, etc. We provide it and you can put your own brand on it."

Another part of *Effortless Mastery* surfaced for him when he presented it to a world-famous singer (I'm not allowed at this time to reveal their identity). "The meeting was so easy because I was so confident in the model, just the feeling of it and what it would do for people. I didn't care whether he went for it or not. I just wanted to share it with him. This is what I do, this is how much fun it could be, and this is what it's going to mean to the people who love you. I was just excited to show them what the possibilities could be." Being involved in a process and not attached to where the process will go. Hello! That's *Effortless Mastery. (Oh well, Buddhism may have come first!)*

"Being stuck on an idea is like being in a box. Now I know the difference between what I think something is and what it really is. Being the guitar player, being on tour because I put so much into this, telling people that's what I am, that's the idea I was in love with, but that idea was not my purpose. I let it go and now I only follow things that I get excited about, excited telling people about, that's the only things I do."

There are so many great lessons in Brian's story. He applied concepts he learned through the study of music and *mastery*. It led him to the fulfillment he had always sought. My hope is that in contemplating the lessons of *Becoming The Instrument* you may be brought to *The Genius Inside*.

24 ■ The Genius Inside

The Genius Inside 1

Dear ones, don't you know there is a genius waiting to create through you? You merely have to step aside and let "It" play. Let It create, then love and appreciate every note It plays.

The Genius Inside 2

Letting "The Genius" come through is a matter of releasing The Genius from the bondage of limitation, much like Michelangelo's concept of "liberating the statue from the marble."

The Genius Inside 3

They say, "As you think, you become. We can all validate that statement from our own experiences. For years we have thought "I am limited by _____" and it has manifested. What would happen if we foolishly declared "I am a master,

I am a genius?" How much greater might we become? And the thing is, whether the statement is true or not, what do have to lose by saying it?

The Genius Inside 4

I have a genius inside me. Now I relax, take a deep breath, and let that genius come through.

The Genius Inside 5

If you accept that there is a brilliant presence inside you that is capable of brilliant actions, it inspires you to achieve mastery over the mechanics.

The Genius Inside 6

Master all the aspects of the music you've chosen to play, let the execution of that music be as effortless as driving to the gig. Then relax, take a deep breath and let It play.

The Genius Inside 7

If there is a Master Musician in all of us, then we roll out the red carpet and invite "It" to speak through us. The red carpet is the intense training we go through in the given subject. I study my subject over and over, the way a monk studies his scriptures, to reduce the technique to muscle memory, intellectually or physically. In this way, virtuosity serves at the feet of consciousness.

25 ■ I Am a Master

In my book *Effortless Mastery,* I have several meditations where I use the phrase, *"I am a Master."* It is one of the least understood parts of the book. I get the question all the time: "How can I be a master when I'm not even a good musician? Aren't I deluding myself?" Perhaps the right phrase would be, *"I have a master inside of me. I surrender to that force now."*

You see, if you identify yourself as a flawed, unworthy entity who lacks light, all your efforts will confirm this view. For example, if you learn to play an instrument with the understanding, "Well, I'm not very talented and I'm already too old to do this but . . ." the results will be as you would have expected. But when you say *"I am a master,"* and realize it at the moment you're about to touch the instrument, that takes an act of faith, something you can't see. You have to have the faith that the same creative force that lies within all great beings lies within you.

Now, if your faith is unshakable, it would be tantamount to confidence; a confidence that is unshakable. You would try things and do things. If one assumes themselves to contain mastery, then it is a question of training the body to express it. If you believe yourself to be a creative entity capable of unlimited expression, you would say, "I haven't learned this lesson yet because *the master isn't able to use it.* You would expect connectivity to your *creative side.* Obviously, if you don't think you have a creative side you wouldn't expect that.

An affirmation is just that, an affirmation. You may have proof of what it says, you may not, but proof or not, you affirm its truth. The bottom line is, those who assume mastery exists within go further in their creative exploits than those who assume their light is duller than others.

As stated a number of times previously, all paths allude to a space within one's own being that is undisturbed by external forces. *That is the master space!* I get challenged by thoughts. Those thoughts don't comfort me at all, quite the contrary. The space is where The Divine and the Light and the Sound all merge. It takes steady self-effort to connect with that kind of clarity in life. But in music . . . *why not?*

Mastery is not perfection, or even virtuosity. It is giving oneself love, forgiving one's mistakes, and not allowing earthly evidence to diminish one's view of one's self as a drop in the Ocean of Perfection. In this sense, *we are all masters. The world is divided into those who know it and those who don't.* It's a leap of faith.

"I am a master" means that mastery lies within you. The only thing lacking may be language or technique. This is true of all pursuits. If you believe it then you will calmly work toward whatever your goal is, but with the awareness that *the Master is already there, waiting for the disciple to acquire the skills.* Do you believe there is a Master, a Creator at your core, at the center of your being? If so, take a breath and let him permeate your entire being now.

"I" is "He." If "He" is a Master, then *I am a master.*

Having gone this far in my journey, I realize:

The only way out is to go forward.

26 ■ Living with Purpose, Playing with Purpose

Your purpose in life is to find your purpose and give your whole heart and soul to it.

/ Gautama Buddha /

Up till now, I think I have pretty much downplayed the importance of music. Let's explore the other side of the coin—how important music can be with purpose. Let's say you have virtuosity; there's another thing you might contemplate, *relevance*. What is your music relevant to? Anything? Is the message, *Hey look at me! Look how clever I am!"* That motive may be enough for you. I wouldn't demean it. Actually, that motive is very common in the more complex art forms of classical music and jazz.

Or your motive may be quite noble. Music for music's sake" or, Art for art's sake." I get it. Early in my career, I might have been motivated by that goal.

Relevance or purpose is not an imperative unless you

think it is, unless you need it to be. Artists of all persuasions could ponder what their work's relevance is to life. What does your music have to do with anything? Is it political, motivated by injustice? Does it inspire others towards greatness? Are audiences put in touch with their Higher Power when they hear you? In other words, *does your music serve a purpose?*

I am reminded of Richie Havens at the Woodstock Festival of 1969. Havens was an ideal choice to play the Woodstock Festival, but he was never meant to have top billing. A traffic jam held up several of the performers and Havens, who was slated as the fifth act, was urged on stage. Three hours later, he ran out of songs and created an enduring anthem on the spot. "When you hear me play that long intro, it's me stalling. I was thinking, 'What the hell am I going to sing?'" he explained. "I think the word 'freedom' came out of my mouth because I saw it in front of me. I saw the freedom that we were looking for. And every person was sharing it, and so that word came out."

"'Freedom' has become the anthem of youth wherever I go," Havens told *Discoveries* magazine in 1994. "But I'll sing it for the rest of my life, if only to show the rest of the world what I think an American is. Sometimes I think we don't know ourselves. But people are all the same, everywhere. They laugh in the same places, even if they don't know the language." Purpose can cause the music to soar beyond music itself.

Andy Statman, who I referred to earlier, played a lot of spiritually charged Jewish religious songs, very chant-like. I believe it was through this medium that Andy spoke to God. He told me a few stories that dramatically illustrate how powerful music can be when it is driven by a purpose larger than itself. "In the Hasidic tradition, the music is considered so deep that it purifies the soul. During the time of the First Temple of Jerusalem there were instrumentalists who would be called on to put prophets into a state of prophecy. If people had committed a certain sin, they would play particular melodies regarding that particular sin and it would 'root the guts' out of the person and totally purify them." He then told me three stories that illustrate the point of this chapter.

Story #1

There was a rabbi, named Rabbi Fastig. He was a member of the Modzitz Hasidic group within Orthodox Judaism, which derives its name from Modrzyce, one of the boroughs of the town of Dęblin, Poland. He was on the cattle cars heading to Auschwitz. The physical conditions were intolerable. We've all seen the pictures. There was no escape from the physical torment of being packed onto those trains in the heat, no ventilation and no water. Rabbi Fastig started to improvise a melody and used words that spoke of complete faith that the Messiah would come, even though he may tarry. He started singing it and then other people were singing it and soon the whole cattle car was singing it. Then all the cars were singing this melody! The Rebbe said to his friends, "I'll give you half my place in heaven if you can somehow escape and get this song to the Modzitza Rebbe. Somehow, two of the Hasidim jumped off the train. One was killed instantly, but the other survived and made it to Switzerland, where he stayed until the end of World War II. Right after the war, someone actually wrote the notes of Rabbi Fastig's song down and it was mailed to America. It got to the Modzitza Rebbe, who had escaped earlier, moving around Europe and coming through China,

Shanghai and Japan, finally ending up in Seattle. Andy and I used to play this song! I'm talking about music that has *that much meaning!*

Story #2

The first Modzitza Rebbe had diabetes. All the great specialists were in Berlin in the 1920s. He went there and they told him that they would have to amputate his leg but at his age they couldn't give him anesthesia. He said that's not a problem. He looked out at the skyline of Berlin and saw how magnificent it was and he started to think about how Jerusalem was in ruins. He started to compose a melody. He went into a trance and composed a thirty-six-part melody. When he finished composing, he came out of the trance and found that the operation was over. Andy claims this story is 100 percent true!

I said to Andy, "Let me ask you a stupid question. For all the worship and practice you do, if you were ever in that situation, do you think you could ever access that state of consciousness?" He said these rabbis are people who have basically been working on themselves since they were born. They have minds that we can't even begin to fathom. They're on such a high level of existence that they can access that any time they want to, or they may be born in that state. (Very much like the gurus and ascetics of India.)

Story #3: Another story about the Alter Rebbe

When the Hasidic movement started, they were controversial because they did things that were innovative in terms of singing and dancing in certain ways, and how they interpreted the teachings. Other Jewish sects were skeptical. The Alter Rebbe was a great scholar of the highest order.

Before he became Hasidic, he studied in the great yeshivas (schools) of Lithuania. He was sent as an emissary to different communities where they were opposing the Hassidim, to explain that what the Hassids were doing was not at odds with formative Judaism. A meeting was set up and he came to it. A lot of the great scholars posed difficult questions to him to see if he was the real thing. Sensing their skepticism, he said that before his sect discussed the Torah, they sing a melody known as a nigun. He closed his eyes and sang one of these melodies and when he opened them, no one had any questions.

———————

March 3, 2020.

Today, I helped one of the students at the Global Institute at Berklee. He is from Colombia. For a final project, he chose to go to the jungle in Colombia and hang out with the musicians there. He said two things that struck me. "For Colombian musicians, music isn't music. Music is life." He asked one of the drummers what the meaning was of the drum he played. He said that the drummer really didn't know how to answer, that trying to express what the drum means is like asking a person, "Who are you?"

Along with the musicians and people from the village, the student was worried that their culture would be wiped out. All such cultures must struggle for survival. Those cultures are nature itself. Climate change and other forces of Western civilization are wiping out so much of nature, I'm afraid these cultures will go along with it.

When you give your life to something, when you dedicate all your gifts to that purpose, it may turn an impressive resume into a purposeful life. When you dedicate all your talent, inspiration, and even your practice, to a cause, you may find more brilliance within yourself. Waves of purpose overwhelm blocks of ego. Performing without purpose can become as tedious as anything else. Your purpose may be to express the darkness of your own soul. No one size fits all. The purpose of your art may be to conquer fear, or to follow your joy or your sorrow. Your life's purpose may be to find peace, embody it, and spread it in your interaction with the world. Perhaps your purpose is to help others shed fear and angst, or even banish disease. That's the promise and the hope. You may never change the world, but *your intention of doing so will change you,* and yes, maybe even the world.

27 ■ Ladies and Gentlemen, Introducing *The Spot!*

In late 2018 I released a CD titled *The Space.* It was the culmination of more than thirty years of identifying *The Space* as the simplest expression of space beyond the conscious mind. While taking a walk today I received a new way to enter *The Space*: **The Spot!**

Have you ever considered that connecting could be ridiculously simple? We're comfortable with the idea that it's harder and trickier than we think, this business of keeping the mind under control, keeping connected to the spirit and staying conscious and mindful. What if God *IHE* made it really easy to join him, and we never saw it? Perhaps he would say, "Hey, know what? I put a button in you—*The Spot.*"

The Spot! Yeah! Imagine there's a God on whom we have superimposed all this meaning. Therefore, we imagine that he superimposes all this *meaning on to us!* (Maybe the supposition of meaning is what weighs us down?) But he says, "Nah . . . no, no. It's very cool! There's a button on your body.

Push it . . . and your troubles are gone. Cool, huh?" (We all know that God speaks more like a jazz musician than a Pope!)

If "The Kingdom of Heaven (*The Space*) lies within you," there must a doorbell and a doorknob. *The Spot!* Where is The Spot? Where is that gate, passageway, or entry point to that space? For me, The Spot is somewhere in my solar plexus. I might put a finger on that area and feel my diaphragm expanding and contracting as I focus on the "doorknob."

The Space is the place, but it may be even more accessible if you visualize a point of entry. Focus your mind on the exact place you breathe from. *That is The Spot!* You can touch that spot and enjoy the expanding and contracting of your diaphragm. *Imagine that's all it takes to entertain you!* Feel the air move as if sliding a silk scarf through your fingers. Now, enjoy!

Imagine walking around, seeing, hearing, even thinking, while concentrating your awareness on the spot. That really greases the runway. While focusing on The Spot, you find that you are "seeing," not "looking," "hearing," nor "listening." While focusing on The Spot you are acting, not wondering what action to take. Like everything else, The Spot takes practice. The mind will seduce one into mental activity, as is its wont. The seduction may be offering great ideas! Play cat and mouse with it and you will receive one great idea after another! When you catch yourself thinking, make a note of the great idea and then touch . . . *The Spot.*

The more one remains focused on The Spot, the more likely one is to remember *The Space* and, without warning, enter it. Then you become sort of like Iron Man: the body is a suit, but the controls lie within. If *The Space* is the sun, The Spot is the magnifying glass. *The Space* is the Promised Land, *The Spot* is the point of entry.

OK . . . I have now focused my awareness on *The Spot*. Each sentence being written right now occurs after I refocus on the doorway. See the door, see the doorknob. Feel it in your solar plexus. Let it begin wherever you feel it. Touch that spot, open that door and enter the world of unlimited space, time, talent, and support. Become your own best friend . . .

OK . . . I'm back . . .

Perhaps you touch that spot and streaks of light course through *The Space* like lightning! Touching one spot ignites the fire of consciousness. Just like the G-spot, or the sweet spot—one touch and you're dwelling in a world of light, color, sound, connection, vibrancy, *Shakti!* Focus on The Spot and plunge into the entire Universe!

The Spot is also a programmable button. You know the instruction booklets you get in the box with computers and other devices? How you can program the buttons for different uses? I am now reading the tiny instructions pamphlet that came in the box with illustrations of what the buttons do. You can program the spot to be a point of relaxation.

Or you can program it to stop thinking. Imagine when you push the button and you steer away from the left fork, the shit hole (technical term for the conscious mind) and towards the right fork, just breathing.

Perhaps you are weighed down with the thoughts of the past or the future. The button can be programmed to zap you right into this moment.

You can program it to be a chanting spot. Push the button and the mantra repeats in your inner ear.

Imagine your breath is God *IHE*. When you push the button, you are instantly with God. The Spot is the focal point leading to the Source. It's the direct route to metaphysical contact.

Find that spot for you, perhaps right in the center of your chest, or right where your heart is. Perhaps for you it is the crown chakra,[1] or any of the chakras. Let your attention stream towards that spot. Visualize a laser to and from that spot, boring a whole through the invisible wall of ego and fear. Stay focused there as your arms move freely, or even wildly, as if they were not under your control, with a mind of their own. Continue to focus on The Spot. Now let yourself move around the room, fast or slow, but keep your attention right there on The Spot. Let everything fly: run, dance, whatever. But keep your eye on The Spot. Take a walk in the garden, but instead of looking at anything, "see" while focusing on that spot. Read, listen to music, but don't listen, *"hear." Be creative!*

The Spot, the doorknob that opens the door to infinity. Imagine a black-and-white world, like in the first part of The Wizard of Oz. When you grab the doorknob and open the door, like Dorothy, you suddenly enter a world of color.

Perhaps you can send messages from that spot, even morse code. You could send blessings to the world, to friends or family, wishes for yourself or others. You can send light through the keyhole. Sometimes, opening the door thrusts you into the world of light. Perhaps you open the door and dive into a clear pool, or be enveloped in sound. Being out of *The Space* can feel like banging on a glass globe and no one is hearing your pleas. Every time you notice your breathing, every time you go to The Spot, you are forging a less travelled neurological passageway into one that becomes more

---

1   The word chakra comes from an ancient Indian language known as Sanskrit. Chakra means vortex, spinning wheel or circle. Chakras are the major centers of spiritual power in the human body and are circles of energy which balance, store and distribute the energies of life all through our physical body along the subtle body.

and more accessible. Let's try it for the rest of the day, whenever you think of it. Whatever, whenever, no matter what's going on, see how many times you can remember to focus on that tiny spot, the keyhole, the doorknob, the door that opens to the heart's desire!

There are other simple things too. I've worked on internalizing a mantra with a sweet melody. I've repeated it so much that it's going on in my head when I'm not thinking of it. It's now a viable alternative to the world of thoughts.

I may wake up thinking, "Ugh, I have to drive here, or I have to go there." I might touch The Spot and take the road less travelled, but increasingly accessible. It's like cutting a groove. The more you groove it, the easier it is to fall into the groove.

The Sun is The Power, I need the magnifying glass to bore a hole through my ego into my soul. Focus your attention on The Spot, and enter *The Space*.

Trust the breath. Touch The Spot, enter The Space.

Maybe it's easier than we think, a simple path for complicated people.

28 ■ Meditation #4
A Dharana[1]

From chapter 24, Comparison of Eastern and Western Thought.

Close your eyes. With eyes closed, keep staring. It seems to be empty, but really is not. Take notice of all the patterns and moving parts on this screen. Allow yourself to become fascinated by it all. Like a large tapestry, there's lots of interwoven images, but it is a moving tapestry. Things in the picture move. Allow yourself to tune into that.

Now, feel the breath move through you. Notice the breath come in, notice it go out. Notice the breath come in, notice it go out. Notice air filling your lungs, notice the release when the air goes out and they empty. Let the eyes continue to observe the tapestry on the screen of closed eyes, and notice the in and out flow of your breathing. Localize your awareness to only these two things, that is the perfect instrument. Stay with this for a while.

---

1   Dharana is the sixth limb of the eight-limbed path as defined by Patanjali, who compiled the Yoga Sutras. Dharana means "holding," "concentration," or "steady focus." When you practice Dharana, you are "binding" the mind to one place, idea, or object. When one is asked to focus with one-pointed focus on ≠, that too can be a dharana.

(Wait two minutes)

Listen to this Story (Dharana)

Imagine a globe. First, you are looking at the globe from a place of great height, perhaps from space. It could also simply be a cartoon of the entire globe. Get an image of the planet. See dots appearing all over the globe, filling the entire globe. We are going to zoom in closer to the globe. The dots are beginning to have more definition. They're not dots, they're people. Now see the entire globe: every continent, every country, every state. See them all filled with standing people.

They're all looking at the sky. But now see them in groups. Each group has a prophecy that tells them their way is The Way.

Now relax and breathe for a few moments . . . imagine the sky with clouds gathering and rolling. Something is hidden behind the clouds as they continue to roll in and fill the sky around the world. Suddenly, from behind these massive white clouds emerges the Great God himself, but all colors, all genders. Their appearance seems to confirm every religious belief on earth. All groups are simultaneously seeing what they always believed God to be.

    Suddenly, this God who appears as someone different to every group, drops his costume. God no longer has any attributes, any details. God is Light. Like the sun, they are nothing but heat and light. After they shed their disguise, everyone is blinded by the light. Now all the people on the earth can see is light. The heat and brightness are unbearable to their conscious minds. Their individual minds disintegrate. All the clothes burn off of them. Every physical part of them burns up in a second, and all that is left of each of them is a column of light. Looking around, they see the people are no longer people, but columns of light. Everywhere they look, like stalks in a cornfield, columns of light.

Now look down at yourself (with closed eyes). Your body has disappeared. All you are is light. Feel light, like a light saber, moving up from the bottom of your feet, up the legs, into the torso, filling the chest, the arms, hands, neck and head. Feel light up and down your spine. Now you are a column of light. Breathe in that column of light and transform more and more into the column of light.

Now let your mind's eye zoom out a bit again so you can see yourself and all the other columns of light around the earth. Breathe . . . Breathe . . . Breathe . . .

Now see all the columns of light merge into one great light. Breathe . . . breathe . . . Breathe . . .

Now see the whole planet merge with that light and the earth has now become a sun. Breathe . . . Breathe . . . Breathe . . .

Now see the "earth sun" merge with the "God sun" that was the sky. Breathe . . .

Now we are all one. We are all light. We are all one light.

Open your eyes and immediately try to do your work or play your instrument with this awareness. Feel the difference . . . Become the instrument!

29 ■ Meet God

One day I was walking through the Muir Woods in Northern California. The redwoods are so huge that they often block sunlight as you walk among them. But as I walked, I reached a clearing where the sun was shining on one particular tree in the clearing. Because of the sunlight this one tree appeared to have silver leaves. There were dust particles around the trees and because of the sunlight they were shimmering. If I were a pre-science man and had seen this tree brimming with light, I might have dropped to the ground and worshiped it. Because of my so-called ignorance I would have had a transcendent experience.

Another time I was on a conference call, which I took sitting in my backyard. It was a cool day in June with a lot of wind. I have big trees in my backyard and I watched them dance while on the call. It was cloudy, and nature was a bit violent that day. On the call someone recited a prayer and just as he did the sun peeked out from the clouds right above the big trees. If I didn't understand fundamental things about sky, clouds, wind, etc., I would have thought that God revealed himself as that prayer was spoken. The question is whether that isn't, in fact, the truth? How we harmonize with our environment is what can be understood as raw, non-dogmatic spirituality. It goes very much to the point of whether life is a series of ordinary or extraordinary moments. It's up to us.

Was early man simply unaware of the science, or did he see things in proper perspective? Maybe that *is* seeing things as they really are. Perhaps small miracles happen every day with unseen synchronicity. On a hot, muggy day, one might have a tender thought and suddenly feel the slightest cool breeze, perhaps a spirit saying, "go with it." You think you've heard the answer to a question on the inside, and the trees suddenly move with the wind. Previously they lay dormant. Maybe the trees were excited about that answer. Which view is correct? More to the point, which would create a life of wonder?

This morning, I saw rows of dandelions growing wildly right outside my studio. They are generally considered weeds, yet they are so pretty. Who's to say they aren't a free gift from The Creator? **Is it God? What God? I don't know. Make one up!** (Repeat the sentences in bold and impose the voice of comedian Jackie Mason) Once you have, pray to *She/He/It/They* with all your heart. You will be rewarded for your efforts. And you will become ***The Instrument.***

And while I'm pontificating on the profundity of early "man," let me point out that the English language uses one gender to describe "mankind." You've seen me struggle with gender language throughout the book. It *is* important. How many thoughts and inspirations did we not hear from God's more useful instruments, women? What truths could we have held to without the folly of male-dominated religiosity, had women been given the pen as well?

The following was received the morning of, July 23, 2019, from the Pure Space without the filter of reasonable doubt.

You can meet God touching a piano. Touch it without thought and without desire. Imagine the touch is like the fresco painting *The Creation of Adam* in the Sistine Chapel. God speaks through the piano and he is waiting for you to press one of the buttons, activate the hammer that strikes the string and *behold!* God sings! You become the conduit that allows witnesses, sometime referred to as "audience," to experience God's voice. That's why on occasion, one note can be a revelation to a room full of people, but no one knows why. This is why. God spoke and we heard. Someone had to press the button. What mercy! What accessibility. How *generous!* Getting my mind in alignment with *The Space,* or my breath, or meditation, I do become a conduit. *If I am open to it.*

If one learns to touch the piano from a place so focused, yet so empty and inviting, one can do it touching anything. We can do it touching each other. Every touch can be *The Creation of Adam.* What about those pesky thoughts? *Receiving thoughts* with no fear, no desire, no failure and no success, could be a day's worth of genius. If one touches the piano and evokes the Creator, *the music becomes irrelevant.* After all, from this perspective, *there are no wrong notes.*

And here is the good news: **You don't have to be a musician to have the experience!**

Another way of looking at the 1st step

Become blank. Become attentive to the eyes of the Lord. (You could be looking in your own eyes!) Stare unto them with complete surrender. Allow the arm to float up in the air towards the keyboard until it hovers over the white keys. Then let the hand descend a bit until all five fingertips are touching the keys. Let that slightest touch be enough to hold the rest of the arm in midair.

Now refocus your attention on your breathing, reconnect your eyes with the horizon. Lift a finger, the thumb of the right hand or the pinky of the left. Hold the finger in the air for a while. In that time, connect even stronger with the breath and the eyes, then—play the note. Allow the finger to realize its connection to the key and allow the note to fill your ears and move through your whole body so that you are filled with God's First Note.

Now let the finger keep a simple contact while no longer sustaining that note. Return to your breath and your gaze, even if you've drifted a little bit. Lift the next finger and hold it in the air while you refresh your attention to the breath and the gaze. God just played the next note.

Move this way, note after note, but don't disregard the possibility that the first note is, and will always be, enough.

When necessary, drop the hand and start over. When the hand returns, start with the next finger. Let all of the fingers get the benefit and the intention of the first finger. Let each note be the first. Let every moment be the first moment. Balance yourself on the head of a pin until it becomes a broad highway that you can easily walk, with room to spare. It's not mystical anymore. It is simply the way you play, who you are. You're being created moment by moment, like Adam, while looking out the window, emptying the garbage, doing your work, or simply being with family.

I would like to quote the great saint of India, Baba Muktananda. He said, *"God dwells within you as you."*
OM Shanti, Shanti, Shanti. Om peace, peace, peace.

■ Epilogue

I was burning through writing this book in December of 2016 and January of 2017, when I was accepted to go to India to the Mother Ashram of the path I follow. This was a great boon and, as with many things, a moment of challenge and fear. I was going in early February. It seemed like the perfect culmination, if you will, to the previous months where I was centered, creative and highly productive. Now it was time to spend more than two weeks doing nothing but focusing on The Self, my heart, God.

It took quite a while to get into the spirit, so to speak. My mind chattered over the din of sublime currents. My predominant thought was, *what the f*** did I come here for?? Trapped in the house of God with no Wi-Fi!"* After six days, the nectar did eventually drown my thoughts and I started to taste it. One day, I went to the local town and heard Brahmin priests chanting all day. Time became timeless. No thoughts! When I got up from my seat, I understood the concept of intoxication. I was bumping into walls. When I returned to the ashram, I was able to resonate much more naturally with the

Shakti, the Goddess energy so named in my faith tradition. I then spent probably the most consistent time I've ever experienced dwelling in *The Space,* rather than struggling with my mind. As I've stated all through the book, this was never the problem in music. But now I was experiencing it in my life. Finally, my life! I left there very much in synch with the Inner Guru, my own Higher Self. I felt like right choices were spoken from within. I just had to listen. Just like with music!

But when I arrived home from India, I became confused. I came home with my sensors wide open. I could have used at least a week to be home, meditate, recopy my notes, and assimilate this scintillating experience. I did not do that. Circumstances around my going, scheduling, other responsibilities were a bit at odds with the trip. I wanted to make sure that if I finally went all that way, I would stay as long as I could. Consequently, I went right back to work. No adjustment period.

There were three competing layers pulling on me. There was business that had accumulated while I was gone, which needed attention. Then there was creative work that had to be done for engagements coming up shortly: performances, recordings, stuff like that. Then there was the thing I actually wanted to do, which was nothing but sit in my studio, meditate, contemplate, and journal. The battle of these three levels really confused me. (I can tell you that if I go again, I will *absolutely* leave time to assimilate!) The confusion was uncomfortable, but not debilitating. I still retained a lot of light and energy from my journey. But then things took a nasty turn.

About a week after returning, I played a gig in Manhattan. The idea was to do two sets, stay in a hotel because I lived so far from NYC, and come home the next morning. Strangely,

I decided to go home that night. And I didn't immediately head for home but hung out another hour. Stranger still was that on my way upstate I stopped for gas, but didn't get coffee. I would have always done that if I were coming home late, not to mention still being on India's time zone. How could I be so careless? What was happening?

I was driving home on Route 17 heading for the Catskills when about five exits from my exit I fell asleep at the wheel. I usually open the window and get fresh air to wake me up, but this time it did no good. I crashed into one guardrail and woke up abruptly, but the car was already bouncing across the road towards the other guardrail. Thank God, the car didn't flip over. It just sort of slid. Also, thank God that at that hour of night there were no other cars on the road.

The car was totaled but I was in one piece. My head was bleeding like a waterfall, which freaked me out, but it didn't actually hurt. I found my phone on the car floor, dialed 911, and told the police where I was. Then I made the call I was dreading, to my wife. She had told me to stay in town, and has told me a thousand times to pull over if I'm tired, and take a nap. I didn't do either of those things. "How many years will it take before I grow up?" I asked myself. This call was all the more dreadful because about ten years earlier she had received such a phone call to tell her that our daughter had died in a car accident. I knew the guru protected me that night, but how did I let this happen?

The policeman who arrived was very nice, very helpful, but then he scared the crap out of me. He wanted to make sure I hadn't been drinking. I assured him I had just fallen asleep at the wheel. But I actually did have a drink at the club before I left. What if I failed the sobriety test? What kind of trouble would I be in then? That would be a whole other kettle of fish! Fortunately, I passed the test. That was the first thing I was grateful for. Surviving the crash was second, believe it or not. When the EMS truck arrived, they stopped the bleeding and said that I wouldn't need stitches. That was the next thing I was grateful for. No sitting in the emergency room all night. I was starting to feel like, all things considered, I was doing pretty well.

Then my wife, Lorraine, came. She was not very compassionate; she seemed to show no emotion. Lorraine is an extremely strong person. She doesn't panic; her father taught her how to face fears and how to survive. I think that was part of my original attraction to her, me being basically the opposite. But she told me the EMS guy could see the fury in her eyes, and I was to find out later what he saw—that if he wasn't there, she would have knocked me out!

I walked away from it, but felt like such a screw up. How could I risk my life this way after all the positive energy I had absorbed in India? How could I be so irresponsible?

I thought I had basically made it through all of this, new car payments aside. Although I hadn't had any lingering physical effects from the accident, a week later I woke up with an acute anxiety attack. Full disclosure, I am no stranger to anxiety attacks, or bouts of depression for that matter. But this was different. I had always experienced anxiety based on worrying about the future. That's what anxiety is, fear of something that hasn't happened yet, may never happen, and all you can do is ruin the day thinking about it. I popped out of bed and sat down to meditate, and that pretty much took care of it. The great practices I did in India delivered me beyond this fearful feeling, to the warmth of the Inner Self.

But it came back the next day, and the next, and many

more after that. Meditation did not take it away, and the fear was so bad, I would sometimes shake. I couldn't possibly do my work—playing or teaching—feeling like this. The book was stopped cold. I had some medications to restore clarity and put the fear at bay so I could function. But every morning it was the same thing—waking up into a storm of fear.

The diagnosis was trauma from the car accident, which is reasonable and common. It could take four to six months to abate. I was in hell every morning. Sometimes, lying in bed, I had to overcome my fear just to get up and wash! How was I going to continue doing my work? This went on month after month. By night I was drinking. I became quite dependent on that drink!

I live in a community of inspired healers, and everyone had a remedy for me. I was overwhelmed with options; enzymes, probiotics, homeopathy, exercise, Hatha Yoga, this shaman, that healer, this therapist, etc. I had been seeing an EMDR therapist for quite a while. EMDR stand for Eye Movement Desensitizing and Reprocessing.

The silver lining of this daily nightmare is that it motivated me to really work on my negative self-image. It caused me to face fears I had had all my life. I chose to see the whole experience, not just as trauma, but as the Shakti working on me to move forward. These *samskaras*, or subtle impressions, could be from early childhood, or even from previous lifetimes.

When I was in India, I became wedded to an idea: *"Trust the breath, trust the Shakti, trust the guru."* It was a thought I had had for many years from my chosen path, but I was never as motivated now. I think the constant pain and anxiety pushed me farther than I wanted to go. They say the

Shakti can cut like a knife. It will change you, but not necessarily pleasantly. Now I was being forced to change. I had looked for refuge all my life. I tried things that gave me a temporary sensations or relief, but the feeling never lasted.

"Trust the breath, trust the Shakti, trust the guru." It seems I am led back to that wisdom again and again. The breath became more central to my mental health as a result of the whole experience: India, the accident, a year of anxiety, and the resulting therapy. It became central to the premise of the book. I knew well how to do this in music. Now I really needed to stay in the moment by watching my breathing. After all is said and done about religion, God and such, it may just come down to that. When I started coming out of it in late 2017, I felt as if I had so much more control over my thoughts, over my fears. I kept experiencing more integration between life and music. Can life be as easy as playing the piano? Can I be as comfortable with the twists and turns as I am with music? Probably not, but maybe . . .

March 16, 2020.

The book is finished!

In the early days of writing, I wrote this at the end of the first chapter:

> It seemed a fortuitous time to finally start my second book, the first one in twenty years, an activity that I suddenly had infinite energy for. I also started writing music again for the first time in a few years. Now I just hoped the world would continue to exist so I could live to enjoy it.

(Now we are in the throes of the pandemic. Hmm, I thought I was just being paranoid.)

———

To musicians everywhere:

Connect with your breath, not your brain. That will catapult you into the Music of the Spheres, the music of your own Heart. It is *your vibrations* that will save the world. I don't know what will be happening in 2046, but if we're still here, it will be because of you. It's time for you to be what you are—emissaries of Universal Consciousness. Musicians, it's time to worship the Higher Power with your sound. It's a wonderful game, sculpting sound into what we call music.

———

Thank you for reading,

KENNY WERNER

Appendix 1
Other techniques for touching The Spot, entering *The Space*

These are a few different exercises that I've found for entering *The Space*.

1. Visualize a space one inch above your head. Keep seeing in your mind's eye the space one inch above your head. Now extend it to two inches above. Stay there for a while. Really try to see two inches above your head in your mind's eye. Feel different?

2. Put your hand flat, one inch above your head. Now move it fast over your head, like you were polishing a surface one inch above your head. Now remove the hand, and see if your sense of that line is stronger where you just had your hand. Do the same with two and three inches.

3. Try to picture the back of your head. Imagine you could "pop out" of the back of your head, and with those eyes observe the back of that head. Now imagine you could "pop out" of the back of that head, and look at the back of the second head. Now back out of that head and see the three heads in front of you. Keep staring at the back of the back of the back of the head. Feel it?

4. Imagine *The Spot* in your solo plexus. In the mind's eye, see that spot and breathe in and out of it. Now touch that spot with one of your hands. Tap the spot. Keep tapping it while watching yourself breathe.

The Center for Enlightened Musicianship

Whether we're jazz, folk, rock or classical musicians, our goal as instructors at the **Center for Enlightened Musicianship** is training individuals to play on higher levels to become channels for a higher purpose. The purpose of all activities will be to awaken the Inner Self, to allow the Inner Self to be the voice of the musician, to Become the Instrument.

We invite people of vision to fund this effort.

About

A board of profound musicians, artists, and business leaders who work together to create a center, an artistic ashram where people evoke their higher selves and convert that into fearless study and performance.

Creating practice methods toward virtuosity—virtuosity serving consciousness.

Courses taught from *The Space* and students listening from *The Space*. One breathing organism.

Create a vibrational choir by first getting in touch with *inner vibration*, the breath, the Shakti, allowing the sound write itself. Later, composers write based on the sounds "received."

Experience spontaneous composition, a new term for free improvisation. An idea built on the assumption that composition is already "written." We practice "hearing" it, surrendering to "It."

Musicians are taught structure and liberation.

Visits from Virtuosos who serve a "divine purpose."

Workshops or retreats that guide seekers towards their own inner mastery.

Effortless Mastery Lectures and Workshops. Piano for non-musicians. Introducing a new somatic discipline to the world *through the striking of one note.*

Sending artists into the world to lift up, not merely entertain. Becoming the strongest force possible to innovate, to initiate, to be a light in a world in desperate need of light.

Changing our collective consciousness means we have to change ourselves.

Acknowledgments

Vivienne Maria Aerts. A sharp, talented and extremely intelligent person. Her determination is a great example for women everywhere. She joined me at Berklee early on and dedicated herself to the success of this institute. I don't know where I'd be without her.

Roger H. Brown. President of the Berklee College of Music. He believed in me very early on and his faith is what coalesced the Effortless Mastery Institute.

Lawrence J. Simpson, Senior Vice President and Provost. For also showing faith that I might be of help to our students and teachers.

Matt Marvuglio. A true visionary. He created the template for the master's program and the Berklee Performance Division Institutes, including Berklee Global Jazz and *Effortless Mastery*. It was his idea to call the institute EMI. He knew what it could become before I did.

Reggie Marshall. My manager and my friend, for selflessly going through every page for mistakes. What a gift he is!

Special thanks to Marc Jaffe, Rob Fried and Bradley Horowitz for supporting me and being an unofficial board of advisors for The Effortless Mastery Institute. They have been very special friends to me.

Jamey Aebersold. The pioneer in Jazz Education who published my first book, *Effortless Mastery*, and changed my life.

The Author

KENNY WERNER is a world-renowned pianist and composer. Werner's collection of compositions, recordings and publications includes his landmark book, *Effortless Mastery: Liberating the Master Musician Within,* which has liberated artists around the world to reclaim their love for music and find the power within their art. In 2014, twenty years after *Effortless Mastery* sold more than 150,000 copies, he became artistic director of the Effortless Mastery Institute at the Berklee College of Music in Boston.

Werner has performed with numerous jazz greats, including Dizzy Gillespie, Joe Lovano, Chris Potter, Ron Carter, John Scofield, Jack DeJohnette and Toots Thielemans. Most recently, he has worked with quintets that have featured Antonio Sanchez, Brian Blade and John Patitucci among many others. In additions to releasing more than 30 recordings, Werner has led and composed for many major international jazz and symphony orchestras. In 2010 he received the Guggenheim Fellowship Award for his seminal work, "No Beginning, No End."

————————

Go to Kennywerner.com/downloads and get Kenny's new meditation tracks.

Made in the USA
Monee, IL
24 November 2023

47198317R10173